NEW RETRO

GRAPHICS & LOGO IN RETRO STYLE

FIRST PUBLISHED AND DISTRIBUTED BY
VICTION:WORKSHOP LTD.

viction:ary™

VICTION WORKSHOP LTD.
UNIT C, 7/F, SEABRIGHT PLAZA, 9-23 SHELL STREET,
NORTH POINT, HONG KONG
URL: WWW.VICTIONARY.COM   EMAIL: WE@VICTIONARY.COM
WWW.FACEBOOK.COM/VICTIONWORKSHOP
WWW.TWITTER.COM/VICTIONARY_
WWW.WEIBO.COM/VICTIONARY

EDITED AND PRODUCED BY VICTION:ARY

CONCEPTS & ART DIRECTION BY VICTOR CHEUNG
BOOK DESIGN BY VICTION:WORKSHOP LTD.

©2016 VICTION:WORKSHOP LTD.
ALL RIGHTS RESERVED. NO PART OF THIS PUBLICATION MAY BE
REPRODUCED, STORED IN RETRIEVAL SYSTEMS OR TRANSMITTED IN ANY
FORM OR BY ANY MEANS, ELECTRONIC, MECHANICAL, PHOTOCOPYING,
RECORDING OR ANY INFORMATION STORAGE, WITHOUT WRITTEN
PERMISSIONS FROM RESPECTIVE COPYRIGHT OWNER(S).

COPYRIGHT ON TEXT AND DESIGN WORK IS HELD BY RESPECTIVE
DESIGNERS AND CONTRIBUTORS. ALL ARTWORK AND TEXTUAL INFORMATION
IN THIS BOOK ARE BASED ON THE MATERIALS OFFERED BY DESIGNERS
WHOSE WORK HAS BEEN INCLUDED. WHILE EVERY EFFORT HAS BEEN MADE
TO ENSURE THEIR ACCURACY, VICTION:WORKSHOP DOES NOT ACCEPT ANY
RESPONSIBILITY, UNDER ANY CIRCUMSTANCES, FOR ANY ERRORS OR
OMISSIONS.

ISBN 978-988-13203-6-0
PRINTED AND BOUND IN CHINA

GRAPHICS & LOGO

NEW RETRO IS A GRAPHIC NOD
TO THE AESTHETICS AND VALUES THAT
WITHSTAND TIME.

NEW RETRO

GRAPHICS

LOGO

MADE IN

RETRO STYLE

Limited Release

NEW RETRO FEATURES IDENTITIES, VISUAL
COMMUNICATIONS, PACKAGING, EDITORIAL AND
INTERIOR DESIGN.

☞ 1st EDITION ☜

ESTD × Design & *Victionary* PUBLISHED × 2016

— FOREWORD —

At a time when the graphic design industry has to deal with a big economic change, our work confronted the change with a contemporary graphic approach using traditional printing techniques that may be considered ancestral for some. We love to keep our hands on a good book or touch a beautiful poster to perceive the subtlety of its print or frame, feel the relief of ink under our fingers and assume that the overprints are there to contribute memorable experiences. We love working with craftsmen who have knowledge and skills in traditional techniques. The sharing and exchange of ideas are very beneficial for the successful completion of our projects.

The "NEW RETRO" emerges when two epochs meet. Our duo devotion to fine prints and creative experiments are combined with the practical knowledge of an able craftsman. By uniting traditional production techniques and mediums with contemporary graphic design, our approach highlights the attractive qualities of printed matter and creates a dialogue in a play on both visual impact and touch.

During the creative process, we devote a lot of time to research paper, printing process and matching colour schemes. A good design may become even better during this set of steps. Sometimes the printing process comes right at the start of our design conception, deriving a design based largely on the technique.

When it comes to our graphic style, our approach is largely drawn on Swiss reductive philosophies, such as Modernism and International Typographic Style. While designers from these movements advocated an accurate focus on the basics without frills for visual efficiency, we also try to bring our own interpretation and global influences our times provide us into our design — influences that naturally come from the multitude of images in the media, internet, the street and museums. By incorporating these influences into subjects represented by their most significant forms, we embrace the age-old principles into modern vocabularies and produce results that are the cleanest and most powerful and relevant to the users ever.

Our interest in combining techniques has been very present across our work, from how we create graphics out of digitalised linocut patterns to the production of our silkscreen posters. When a balanced design is achieved, there's where the peak of perfection lies — when graphics guided with programmed rules is matched with imperfection brought about by an old typographic machine.

THE "NEW RETRO" EMERGES WHEN OUR DUO DEVOTION TO FINE PRINTS AND CREATIVE EXPERIMENTS ARE COMBINED WITH THE PRACTICAL KNOWLEDGE OF AN ABLE CRAFTSMAN.

— A3 Studio —

THE KNOWLEDGE OF THE VISUAL FORM OF RETRO ELEMENTS AND ITS HISTORY, TOGETHER WITH THE UNDERSTANDING OF THE CONTEXT OF THE PROJECT ARE TWO VITAL PARTS OF THE EQUATION.

— Foreign Policy Design Group —

— FOREWORD —

Retro:. /ˈretrō/. Adjective

Imitative of a style, fashion, or design from the recent past.*

The etymology of the word retro is the abbreviation of rétrograde 'retrograde'. Retrograde means going back in time or position.

Design, art, film, theatre, story telling – all forms of creative endeavours entail the process of inspiration, invention and creation. As creatives, we are wired to instinctually and quickly get our hands and brains around anything we find inspiring or suitable for the context of what we are designing for. We research, learn, and then perhaps tweak or simplify or deconstruct or simply re-apply the style wholesale to our work. Sometimes we just collect, archive and hoard any kind of materials we come across like what geeks do and wait to use them one day. (The truth, and you know it, is actually we cannot wait to use them in a project right away!) Such sources of inspiration many times come from elements or style from the past. Human beings are basically a pretty sentimental lot – we have an innate tendency to like that fuzzy warm nostalgic experience, whether we ourselves had actually lived through it or not. We are inclined to enjoy recalling and fitting those experiences into our current ones. We, creatives, love to jolt these memories and evoke these emotions; we like to re-create that moment and re-apply or adapt it to our modern culture and contemporary lifestyle. We believe that our audience will respond to that and enjoy that moment as well.

When we were working on the branding for restaurant HayMarket in Hong Kong, the city being an ex-British colony immediately came to us as something we could hark back to using colonial era graphics. The Hong Kong Jockey Club, the historic colonial building where HayMarket is nestled, gave us further nostalgic elements to play and layer with. We were inspired by the colours and patterns from jockey silks, vintage British typography and Victorian-style illustrations from old advertisements. These ingredients came together perfectly as a great cocktail of quirky and eccentric British traits that aptly suited HayMarket's brand.

It is necessary to apply retro or vintage visuals with care especially these elements are associated to a certain story and experience in time. It is therefore critical to get a crisp understanding of these historical background before any sort of application. The results would be very neat if executed appropriately to the context and concept. However, sometimes we do have to re-adjust the visual language to befit our storyline so that it connects to the current culture for the audience to be more emotionally attached to the brand.

The same applies to the choice of typefaces. Just like Blackletters, also sometimes known as Gothic, Fraktur or Old English, which is a script used throughout Western Europe from circa 1150 through to the 17th century, characterised by its dramatic thin and thick strokes and sometimes the elaborate swirls on the serifs, created based on early manuscript lettering. Blackletter was used in one of the first printed books, Gutenburg Bible, written in Latin and massively reproduced with movable types. But they can become extremely difficult to read as a body text throughout an entire page. An actual example that appeared in the menu of a medieval-style restaurant in Bratislava, Slovakia, when Blackletter was used for the description for each menu item, set in four different languages with diacritics in the Slavic languages. This meant the reader has to seek out for his/her language amongst the stacks. However it will be a totally different picture if the designer of the menu had considered using the Blackletter simply as a header and sub-headers while adopting a more legible font for the food description, a font that is complementary to Blackletter. That way this will aid legibility while still being capable of retaining that medieval feel.

In essence, the knowledge of the visual form of retro elements and its history, together with the understanding of the context of the project are two vital parts of the equation when concocting that cocktail using vintage elements as an ingredient – the appropriateness lies in the hands of the designer.

* "Retro" Def. 1. *Oxford American Dictionary*, Oxford University Press, n.d. Web. 25 Jan. 2016.

✶ RETRO IN ICON ✶

BE IT TYPOGRAPHY-BASED DESIGN OR PURE GRAPHICS, THESE LOGOTYPES AND EMBLEMS EPITOMISE HOW AGE-OLD AESTHETICS ADDS VALUE TO MODERN DESIGN IN SMALL DIMENSIONS. GROUPED NEATLY BY THE NAME OF RESPECTIVE DESIGNERS, AND ARRANGED BY FORM AND STYLE, THIS GOODLY COLLECTION OF LOGO MARKS SHOWCASES THE DIVERSE EMBODIMENT OF VINTAGE LETTERFORMS, GRAPHICS AND ICONOGRAPHY THAT SOLIDIFY THE CONNECTION OF A BRAND WITH THE GLAMOROUS PAST. A UNIFIED MONOCHROMATIC SHOWCASE ACCENTUATES THE INTRICATE STRUCTURE AND GRAPHICAL DETAILS OF THESE MINIATURE DESIGNS.

P. 010 ———— P. 095

NEW RETRO — ICON

ESTUDI ÀLEX RAMON MAS

1

2

3

4

5

6

7

1. Austin & Austin Café, Bar & Lounge   2. Genuine Articles   3. Leonart Motorcycles   4. Motos Hernández
5. Trackswear Vinyl & Wood Sunglasses   6. Ristorante Pizza di Piero   7. The Cigar Company

NEW RETRO — ICON

ESTUDI ÀLEX RAMON MAS

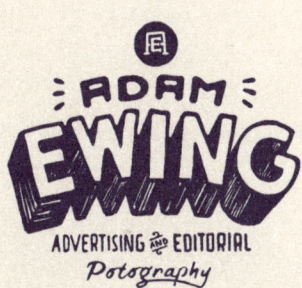 

Adam Ewing Advertising & Editorial Photography

NEW RETRO — ICON

ESTUDI ÀLEX
RAMON MAS

1

2

3

4

5

6

7

8

1. Ars Magna Antiques   2. Astoon Tattoo Studio   3. Moto Kickstart   4. Iron & Air Magazine   5. Joel Gott Wines
6. Crd Café Racer Dreams   7. Ristorante Piazze d'Italia   8. La Gran Tasca Restaurant & Bar

NEW RETRO — ICON

ESTUDI ÀLEX RAMON MAS

1

2

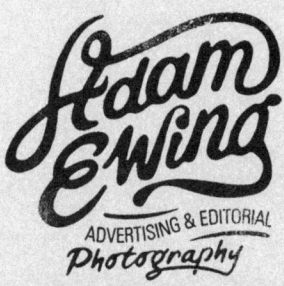

3

4   5

1. Monegros Cycles 2. Fox Racing 3. Adam Ewing Advertising & Editorial Photography
4. Oily Rag Clothing Co. 5. Tazza d'Oro National Barista Championship

NEW RETRO — ICON

ESTUDI ÀLEX
RAMON MAS

Motos Hernández

NEW RETRO — ICON

ESTUDI ÀLEX
RAMON MAS

1

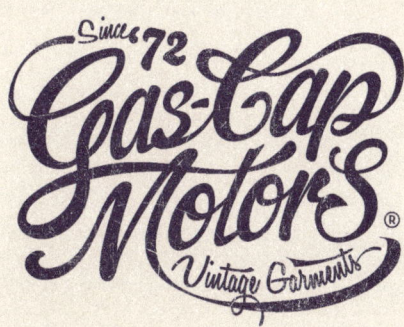

2

1. Pure&Crafted Festival
2. Gascap Motors

NEW RETRO — ICON

ESTUDI ÀLEX RAMON MAS

Gascap Motors

NEW RETRO — ICON

ESTUDI ÀLEX RAMON MAS

Gascap Motors

NEW RETRO — ICON

ESTUDI ÀLEX
RAMON MAS

1

2

1. Gascap Motors
2. Oily Rag Clothing Co.

NEW RETRO — ICON

ESTUDI ÀLEX RAMON MAS

1

2   3

4

1. The Three Thieves Winery 2. Monegros Cycles
3. Crd Cream Motorcycles 4. Harley-Davidson Motorcycles

NEW RETRO — ICON

ESTUDI ÀLEX RAMON MAS

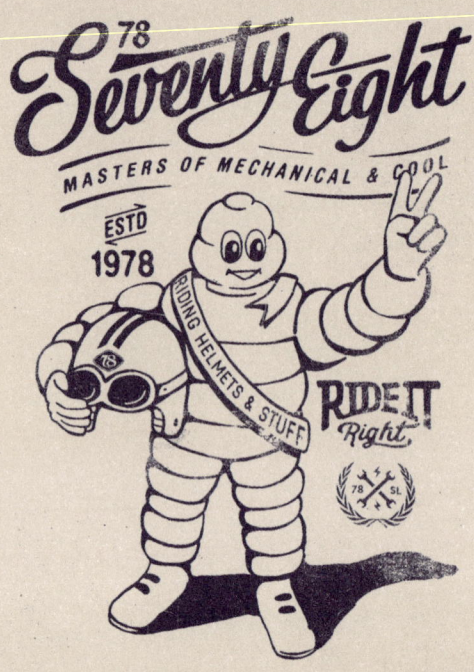

1

2

1. Seventy Eight Motor Co.
2. Crd Café Racer Dreams

NEW RETRO — ICON
Estudi Àlex Ramon Mas

Crd Café Racer Dreams

NEW RETRO — ICON

ALANA LOUISE, COLIN MILLER

1

2

3

1. Wolf Tooth – Ride With the Pack by Alana Louise
2. Bayardstown Big Bottle by Colin Miller   3. Johnny Cash Day 2015 by Colin Miller

NEW RETRO — ICON
COLIN MILLER

1 2

3 4

5 6

1. Humble Hand 2. Proper Knot 3. Studio A.M.
4. Made in Pittsburgh 5. Look Up More 6. This Is A Fire Door

NEW RETRO — ICON
COLIN MILLER

OWN TO TRADE
MOTO
ROSTER
TRADE TO OWN

1

2 3 4

1. Moto Roster 2. Hop Star 3. Look Up More 4. Northeastish

NEW RETRO — ICON

THE GOOD FOLKS CO.

1

2

3

4

5

6

1. Remember Superica   2. Superica Kitchen Tee   3. RocketFit Field Division
4. Commonplace Pocketknife   5. The Good Folks Co. Square Knot   6. RocketFit Squad

NEW RETRO — ICON
DAVID CRAN

1

2

3

4

5

6

7

8

1. Corner Market 2. Tamarack Homes 3. Oxford House Bed and Breakfast 4. Quilchena Cattle Company
5. Lehome Vintage Furniture 6. Atomic Coffee Roasters 7. Black Hole Beer Company 8. Rocket Slide Films

NEW RETRO — ICON
DAVID CRAN

1

2

3

4

5

6

7

8

1. Hewsons Hardware 2. Deuce Cafe 3. Jalopy Journal 4. Jukebox Print
5. Rays Lawn Care 6. Jakes Homestyle Restaurant 7. Johnny's Speed Shop 8. Danny Boy Beer Works

1

2

3

4

5

6

7

8

1. Crisp & Co.   2. Early Bird Espresso & Brew Bar   3. Waterways French Bistro   4. Tazito World Burrito
5. Detroit Ham & Corned Beef Co.   6. Glades Brewing Co.   7. Cotton Company   8. BYDFAULT

NEW RETRO — ICON
DAVID CRAN

1

2

3

4

5

6

7

1. Red Hill Collision Repair 2. Art Bergmann 3. Iron & Air Magazine 4. Red Bomber Productions
5. Side Car Coffee Roasters 6. Vinnie's Restaurant 7. Highflyers Public House

NEW RETRO — ICON

WING'S ART AND DESIGN STUDIO

1

2

1. 1950s Storefront logos
2. Deco Dolls Make-up and Hairstyling

-030-

NEW RETRO — ICON

WING'S ART AND DESIGN STUDIO

1

2

1. Gordano Home Front   2. Travel labels

-031-

NEW RETRO — ICON
MONOTYPO STUDIO

1

OYSTERS & CO

BAR/ BEER AND GRILL

2

1.Cecilia de Quiroz 2.OYSTER´S & CO

-032-

NEW RETRO — ICON
MONOTYPO STUDIO

1

2

3

4

5

1. PIG'S PEARLS 2. Dionnysius 3. ROMEA
4. RIVADAVIA 5. Ofelia Villaseñor

-033-

NEW RETRO — ICON
MILOS
MILOVANOVIC

1

2   3

1.Stolthed Royal 2.Tommy's Guns 3.Khan - The Conqueror

NEW RETRO — ICON

MILOS
MILOVANOVIC

LOUCOMOTION

IMAGERY LAB & APPS FACTORY

Since 2014

1

EMPEROR'S BREWING
Handcrafted Ales and Lagers
—— BREWED IN BELGIUM ——

EMPEROR'S BREWING
Handcrafted Ales and Lagers
—— BREWED IN BELGIUM ——

2

1. Loucomotion Imagery Lab & Apps Factory
2. Emperor's Brewing - Handcrafted Ales and Lagers

NEW RETRO — ICON

MILOS MILOVANOVIC

1. Ponoi River Co. 2. Chickadee Sweets
3. Mill City Fineries Handmade Bow Ties 4. Catalina Candles

-036-

NEW RETRO — ICON

MILOS MILOVANOVIC

NOBLE FARMER
ORGANIC FARMING

1

SIMONSON
LUMBER & HARDWARE

2

1. Noble Farmer   2. Simonson Lumber & Hardware

NEW RETRO — ICON

MILOS MILOVANOVIC

1

2

3

4

1. The Captain's Daughter   2. Caravel Brewing Company
3. Nakua Coffee   4. McArthur Ranch

NEW RETRO — ICON

MILOS
MILOVANOVIC

1

2

3

4

1. Emmu Bottom Homestead - Anzac Biscuits   2. Mad Sons Pub
3. 1776 Effects   4. Muzzle Loaders

NEW RETRO — ICON
GEYSER

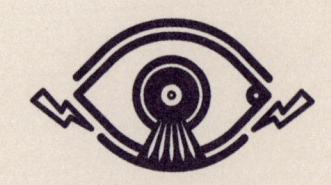

Marks & badges

NEW RETRO — ICON
GEYSER

- Don't count the days, make the days count
- Comparison is the thief of joy 
- Greatness has to be Earned 
- You are Capable of anything 
- Hustle Harder 
- To win you have to Risk Loss 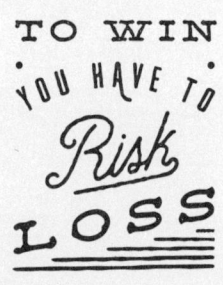
- You win some, you lose some — it's all part of the Game called Life 
- We musn't Dwell on the Negative 
- Try to Encourage yourself & others 

Motivational quotes

-041-

NEW RETRO — ICON
SUNDAY LOUNGE

1. Double Dutch Farms 2. Grit & Thistle Film Company 3. Wild Woods Brewery
4. Guadalupe Brewing Co. 5. SubCulture Cyclery 6. Vino Salida

NEW RETRO — ICON
SUNDAY LOUNGE

1. Drink Local   2. Colorado Boy Pub & Brewery   3. River's Edge Brewing Co.
4. Caveman Brewing Co.   5. Fate Brewing Co.   6. Elevation Beer Company®   7. Colorado Sky Brewing Co.

NEW RETRO — ICON
SUNDAY LOUNGE

1

2

3

4

5

1. Big Beach Brewing Co. 2. Seasons Café 3. Obscure Brewing Co.
4. March Hare Brewing Co. 5. Becky Hersch Hair Studio

-044-

NEW RETRO — ICON
SUNDAY LOUNGE

1. Montanya Distillers 2. Scottsdale Brewery
3. Salida Guitar Expo

NEW RETRO — ICON
SUNDAY LOUNGE

1. Young Life 2. Yolo apparel graphics
3. Salida Hydroponic Supply 4. Wanderlust Festival

NEW RETRO — ICON
SUNDAY LOUNGE

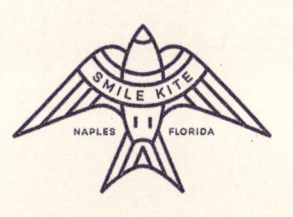

1. Colorado Brewers Rendezvous
2. Smile Kite School 3. Sunday Lounge

-047-

NEW RETRO — ICON
SUNDAY LOUNGE

BARNETT & SON
BREWING Cº
ESTB 2013

BARNETT AND SON BREWING Cº
PARKER, COLORADO

PARKER · BARNETT AND SON BREWING Cº · COLORADO

BARNETT AND SON BREWING Cº
PARKER, COLORADO

BARNETT AND SON BREWING Cº
PARKER, COLORADO

1

GUIDESTONE
EST. 2007
COLORADO

FARMHANDS
GUIDE · STONE
EDUCATION PROGRAMS

FARM to SCHOOL
GUIDE · STONE
GROWING HEALTHY

LANDLINK
GUIDE · STONE
COLORADO

2

1. Barnett & Son Brewing Co.   2. Guidestone Colorado

-048-

NEW RETRO — ICON
SUNDAY LOUNGE

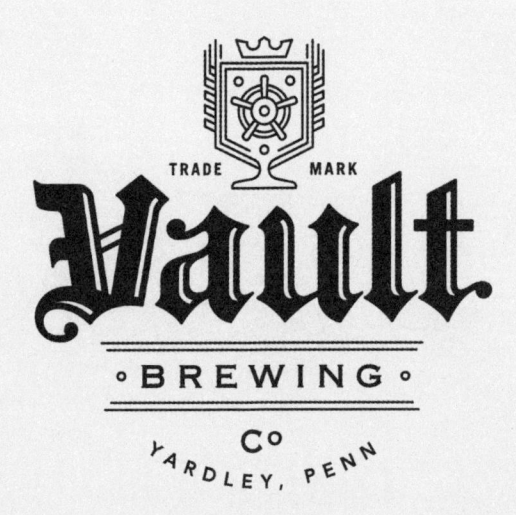

Blindsight
SALIDA · COLO
BREWING

1

Becky Hersch
HAIR · STUDIO
"A cut above"

2

TRADE · MARK
Vault
· BREWING ·
Co
YARDLEY, PENN

VAULT
· EST · 2012 ·
BREWING · COMPANY
YARDLEY, PENN.

3

1. Blindsight Brewing 2. Becky Hersch Hair Studio
3. Vault Brewing Company

-049-

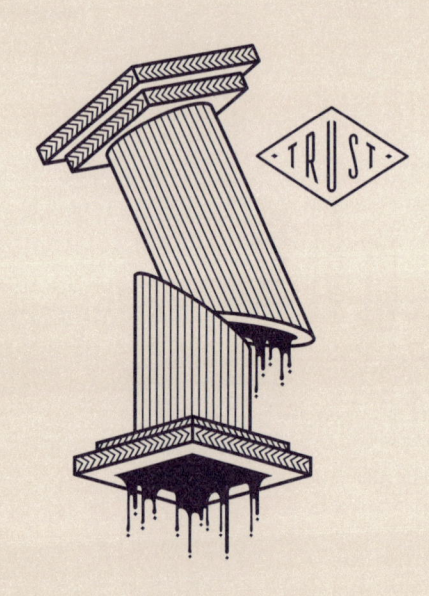

NEW RETRO — ICON
SAY WHAT
STUDIO

Trust the Buzz

NEW RETRO — ICON

SAY WHAT STUDIO

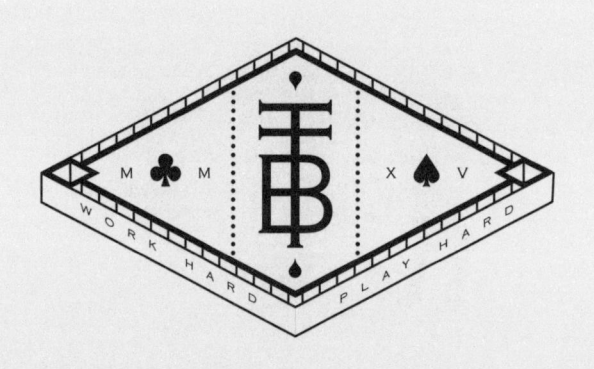

Trust the Buzz

NEW RETRO — ICON
OPUS NIGRUM

SAN **Francisco** CALIFORNIA

THE **HUNTER** DONT LIVE IN THE **Woods**
THE REAL HUNTER LIVES IN THE CITY

the **BEAR** smell the WOODS on the WILD SIDE **WALK**

MAINE **PINE TREE** STATE

BOULEVARD MICHIGAN
THE **Chicago**
RANDOLPH STREET
1979

BLACK PANTHER SOCIETY
WALKING ON THE **WILD SIDE**
SINCE MMXIV

STANDING BUFFALO
THE **Black Foot**
17 80

The **BUFFALO** St Ranch Co. 79 Kansas

American Vintage Badges Part Two

NEW RETRO — ICON
OPUS NIGRUM

American Vintage Badges Part Three

NEW RETRO — ICON

OPUS NIGRUM

American Vintage Badges Part Four

NEW RETRO — ICON
OPUS NIGRUM

THE LUMBERJACK CO
Blue Ridge — North Carolina 1969
MOUNTAINS
- A LIFE AMONG THE EVERGREENS -

WILD TERRITORY
The STRONG BEARS ©
MOUNTAINS

GREY WOLF HUNTER
OUTDOOR
- THE -
LONELY WOLF BROSS
ADVENTURE
MISSISSIPI
- STORE -

- YELLOWSTONE PARK -
THE HOUSE OF
THE American Buffalo CO.
IDAHO   MONTANA   WYOMING

IN A WORLD
THAT'S
CHANGING
I'M A
Stranger
IN A
STRANGE LAND
WHO AM I
to
DECIDE
- WHAT SHOULD BE DONE -

THE
TRAVELERS
NORTH to SOUTH   DUCKS   SOUTH to NORTH
1975   CO.
ESTB   SEARCHING   BROS
A NEW DESTINY

American Vintage Badges Part Five — Native Edition

NEW RETRO — ICON

Opus Nigrum

STRONG IN THIS -LIFE-
Fighting Grizzly
FREE FOREVER
UNTIL THE END

HALCON FREE Co.
7 5
- UNTIL THE END -

-HEAR THE TREES-
LUMBERJACK Co.
19 75
- WORKER OF THIS LAND -

— IN THE —
DESERT *of Life*
I FIND MYSELF
— ARIZONA —

-THE BRAVE NATIVE-
— The —
AMERICAN
75 Co.
BISON
- OWNER OF THIS LAND -

American Vintage Badges Part Six — Native Edition

NEW RETRO — ICON
OPUS NIGRUM

1. Americano typeface   2. American Forkball typeface

NEW RETRO — ICON

ZDUNKIEWICZ STUDIO

"THEY DON'T WANT THE CLASSIC HORROR FILMS ANYMORE."

Bela Lugosi
(1882-1956)

Bela Lugosi

NEW RETRO — ICON
ZDUNKIEWICZ STUDIO

LOKAL.BISTRO
· SLOW FOOD FAST ·

WOLFFE
INDUSTRIES
FORM & FUNCTION

1

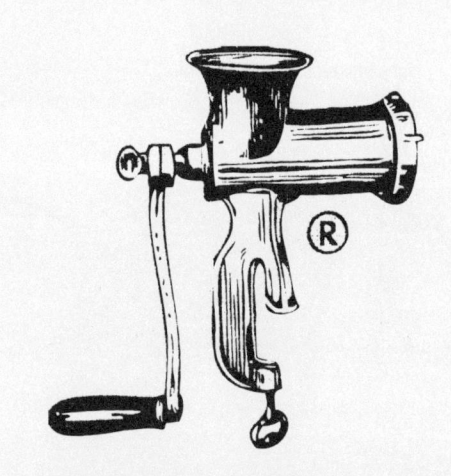

2

1. Lokal.Bistro® 2. Wolffe

-059-

NEW RETRO — ICON
TOBIAS SAUL

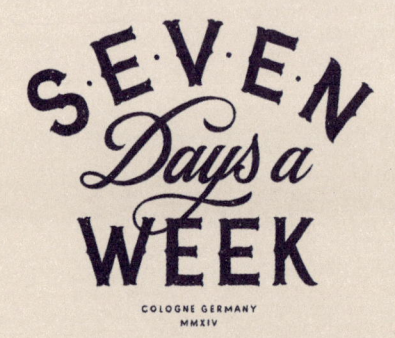

Seven Days a Week Print Shoppe

NEW RETRO — ICON

TOBIAS SAUL

Seven Days a Week Print Shoppe

-061-

NEW RETRO — ICON
TOBIAS SAUL

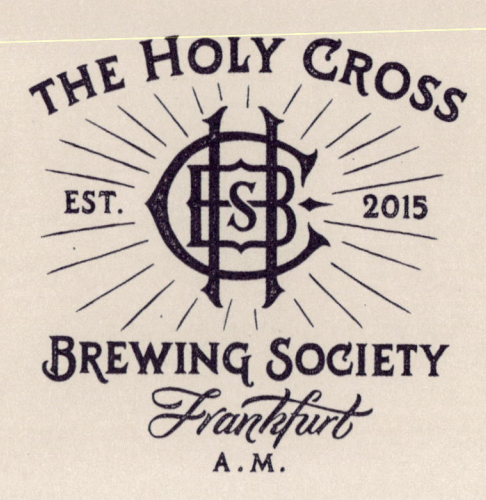

The Holy Cross Brewing Society

-062-

NEW RETRO — ICON
TOBIAS SAUL

1. The Studio at Climber's Rock 2. Stoff aus Frankfurt
3. Wasted Steel on Wheels 4. Seven Days a Week Print Shoppe

NEW RETRO — ICON
DIANA OROZCO

GRAPHIC DESIGN
CALIFORNIA
STEVEN
freelancer

Exclusive Shop
STREET
EST. NEW YORK 2020
PREMIUM STYLE
MADE IN UNITED STATES

RETRO VINTAGE STYLE
blacksuit
CLOTHING
INTERNATIONAL BRAND

THE COFFEE SHOP ★
The Retro
RESTAURANT
New York

BEST FOOD AND BEER
SINCE 2020
Grill Bill
HAVE FUN AND EAT
TEXAS

FREELANCER
David Roth
PREMIUM STYLE
MADE IN UNITED STATES

New York
LAURA DEFELICE
FASHION DESIGNER
a way of living

BLUE SKY
DAVID PETTERSON
AWESOME STYLE
Vip Only

Vintage logos & labels

NEW RETRO — ICON
DIANA OROZCO

CHANDLER
PHOTOGRAPHY
EST. 2020

Photography
JESSICA
ANDERSON
EST. 2020

VINTAGE STYLE
EST. 2020
YARD
exclusive
NEW YORK

Designer
GEORGE
— LUXURY —
new york

Vip Only
KINGSTONE
BEER AND DRINKS
THE PREMIUM STYLE

THE COFFEE SHOP
MICHAEL JONES
RESTAURANT
london

EST. 2020
RESTAURANT
Don Julio
BEER AND DRINKS
PREMIUM

Los Angeles
EST. **MONTES** 2020
LUXURY CLOTHING
modern design

Vintage logos & labels

NEW RETRO — ICON
DIANA OROZCO

THE EXCLUSIVE PROJECT
RETRO GROUP
UNITED STATES PROJECT
FUTURE BRAND

RETRO HOUSE
Vintage
EST. 2020
THE HOUSE OF YOUR DREAMS

EST. 1984
THE MARKET
VINTAGE

NEW YORK
THE VINTAGE APPLE
RESTAURANT

THE AMERICAN BADGE
Exclusive
EST. 2020
CLEVELANT
VINTAGE
CLOTHING

EST. 2020
MEAT AND BEER

Collection
HALFSIDE
CLOTHING
EST. 2020

THE CASTLE
EST. 1984
RETRO STYLE

Vintage logos & labels

NEW RETRO — ICON
DIANA OROZCO

RETRO VINTAGE DESIGN
PREMIUM
EST. 1984
VINTAGE
NEW YORK

EST. 2020
THE WAVES
ENGLAND
RETRO VINTAGE STYLE

THE RETRO WINE
EST. 1984
MADE IN LONDON

RESTAURANT
DALLAS
SPORTS & DRINKS
MILLENIUM

TRADITIONAL LIFESTYLE
RETRO BAR

ENTERTAINMENT
A
BEST NIGHTLIFE

RETRO VINTAGE DESIGN · RETRO VINTAGE DESIGN · RETRO VINTAGE DESIGN · XXL · RETRO VINTAGE DESIGN
NEW YORK
PASSPORT
CLOTHING

ROADS
LA RETRO VINTAGE CO.

Vintage logos & labels

-067-

NEW RETRO — ICON
DIANA OROZCO

TECH AGENCY
SINCE 2020
TECHNOLOGY AND IDEAS

HIPSTER STYLE
EST. 1984
VINTAGE BADGE

BEAT
SOUND
EST. 2020

BEST NIGHT
SHOWTIME
LOS ANGELES

SINCE 1982
OURCOFFEE
RESTAURANT

RETRO
HARRIS
YOU CAN FEEL IT
VINTAGE

EST. 2020
XV
COLLECTION

EST.
THE
VINTAGE
BADGE

Vintage logos & labels

-068-

NEW RETRO — ICON
DIANA OROZCO

Premium
LEONARD
VINTAGE
EST. 1958
ON TOP OF THE WORLD

EXCLUSIVE CHEF
BRIDGET
Tankian

EST. 1984
Carlson
PROFESSIONAL
NEW YORK

EST. 1958
RETRO VINTAGE STYLE
DANIEL JNX
Adventure

THE EXCLUSIVE RETRO VINTAGE BADGE
PREMIUM
LUXURY CORP.
EXCLUSIVE PLACE
NEW YORK
EST. 1982
MADE IN UNITED STATES OF AMERICA

LONDON
THE EVENT
CLASSIC

TAKE ME TO THE SKY
WAITING TO START
AMPLIFY
EST. **THE GROUP** 2015
CLOTHING
VINTAGE PREMIUM STYLE
WORLD INTO ONE
EST. 2015

LOS ANGELES
EST. **CLARITY** 1984
CLOTHING

Vintage logos & labels

-069-

NEW RETRO — ICON
BRIAN STEELY

1. Monster Children Magazine 2. Dashing & Co. 3. Local Wolves Wine
4. The Sheepdogs 5. Pemberton Music Festival 6. Phish Fall Tour 2014

-070-

NEW RETRO — ICON
BRIAN STEELY

1. Newport Folk Festival 2. Morphē Jewelry 3. Phish Summer Tour 2015
4. The Hand & Eye 5. Black Wolf Press 6. Mumford & Sons

NEW RETRO — ICON
BRIAN STEELY

WRKSHOP
BROOKLYN
2016

ESSENCE MUSIC

RAM CUSTOMS

AUDAX SUISSE
DIABLES RANDONNEURS ROUGES

ESTD 2005
THE FRAME THEORY

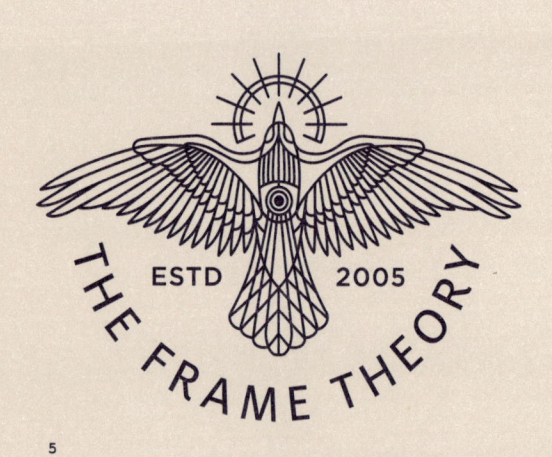

1. WRKSHOP 2. Essence Music 3. RAM Customs
4. Audax Suisse Cycling 5. The Frame Theory

NEW RETRO — ICON
BRIAN STEELY

1

2

3

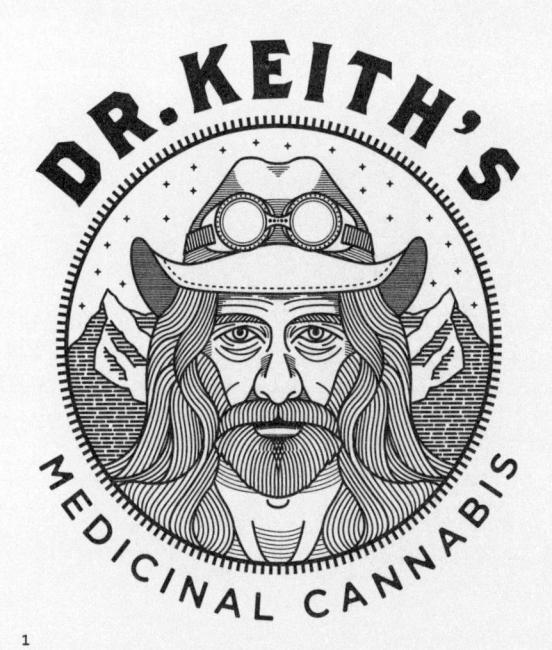

4

1. Dr. Keith's Medicinal Cannabis 2. The Good Doctor
3. The Decemberists 4. Josh Ritter

NEW RETRO — ICON
BRIAN STEELY

CROW THIEF
EXCELSIOR GARMENTS · SAN DIEGO, CA

1

SAD CAT
BLUES BAR

2

INDIAN GARDENS · SEDONA, AZ · EST. 1948

3

RUTHSTEAM ADVENTURE BUDDIES
EST. 2008
WE CAN DO

4

1. Crow Thief 2. Sad Cat Blues Bar 3. Indian Gardens
4. Ruthsteam Adventure Buddies

NEW RETRO — ICON
BRIAN STEELY

1. Owl & Lark Coffee & Juice Bar 2. Adam Snow 3. Arawak Cycles
4. Roupala 5. Sly Loris Hot Sauce 6. Brian Steely personal branding

NEW RETRO — ICON
DOCK 57

1

2

3

4

5

6

7

8

1. Nash Garage 2. Not All Who Wander Want to be Found 3. Hobo and Sailor 4. The Bean Shop
5. Coffee Bob Cafe 6. Jim Aero 7. Black Fox Press 8. Bonaci Seafood

-076-

NEW RETRO — ICON

DOCK 57

EXTRA t-shirt illustrations

NEW RETRO — ICON
DOCK 57

Scandinavia Club

SCANDINAVIA
CLUB

Scandinavia Club

NEW RETRO — ICON

DOCK 57

Scandinavia Club

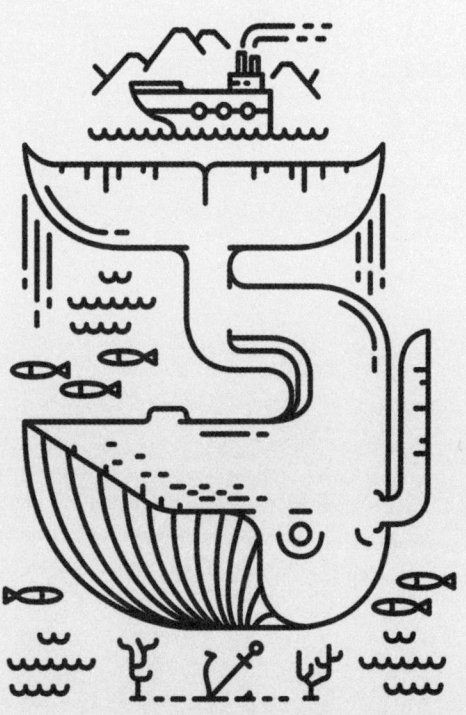

NEW RETRO — ICON

MONOTYPO STUDIO

Isadora

LO PRECIOSO // DE LO VIL

ABCDEFG
HIJKLMNÑ
OPQRSTU
VWXYZ&
1234567890

Clásica, humanista...

orgánica, limpia

Isadora Calligraphy typeface

NEW RETRO — ICON
MONOTYPO STUDIO

Isadora Calligraphy typeface

NEW RETRO — ICON

MONOTYPO STUDIO

CALIFORNIA

1 2 3
4 5 6
7 8 9

CALLIGRAPHIC FONT

Isadora Calligraphy typeface

NEW RETRO — ICON

MONOTYPO STUDIO

Isadora

CALLIGRAPHIC FONT

lo precioso de lo vil...

Isadora Calligraphy typeface

NEW RETRO — ICON
TOM GRUNWALD

1

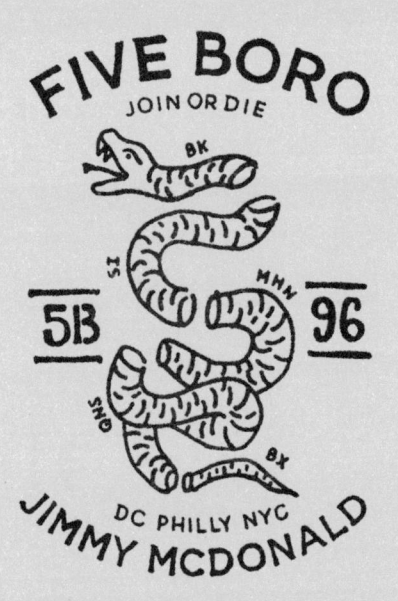

2

3

1. 5Boro Cinco Barrios II   2. 5Boro Don't Tread
3. 5Boro Jimmy McDonald City Hall Pro

-084-

NEW RETRO — ICON
TOM GRUNWALD

1

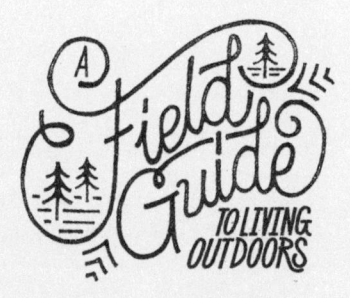

2

1.5050 Skatepark aloha t-shirt 2.Field guide type

NEW RETRO — ICON
TOM GRUNWALD

American traditional tattoo flash — blue print

NEW RETRO — ICON

TOM GRUNWALD

American traditional tattoo flash - letterpress

NEW RETRO — ICON
TOM GRUNWALD

1. Random logos 2. Nuklheads New York

NEW RETRO — ICON
TSENG KUO-CHAN

1.International Children's Games 2.Walk in Tainan
3.Good Days in Kyoto 4.Good Walk from Tainan to Kyoto

NEW RETRO — ICON
ODDDS

THE ANOMALOUS
RARE OCCURANCES

SOULLESS
· CORPSES ·

GODS IN
· MYTHOLOGY ·

EGYPTIAN
· BLACK ·

TALES OF
· FOLKLORE ·

The Anomalous

NEW RETRO — ICON
ODDDS

DWELLERS OF
· VIKING'S DEEP ·

TRAILS OF THE
· WOODSMEN ·

MEDIEVAL
· THRONES ·

THE KINGDOM OF
· ANCIENT ROME ·

NATIVE
· MOTHER ·

The Anomalous

NEW RETRO — ICON
VACALIEBRES

1. Goofle 2. Nuevo México 3. Los Pollos Hermanos 4. Marco Gadau
5. Steph Curry 6. Oca Handcraft

NEW RETRO — ICON
VACALIEBRES

ESTD - 013
PETTIROSSO
HANDCRAFT
GE - IT

1

TX USA
DIMI ARHONTIDIS
IN
EST **MOTUS** 20
VERITAS 14
— STORYTELLING

2

HEY — YOU
PROMOTE
GIVE VOICE AT YOUR MESSAGES

3

GAMBERO

4

DAREK NOVAK
WEDDING PORTRAIT

5

The
PENGUIN
SOCIETY

6

BOSCO dei **CERRI**

7

1.Pettirosso Handcraft 2.In Motus Veritas 3.Promote
4.Gambero 5.Darek Novak 6.Penguin Society 7.Bosco dei Cerri

NEW RETRO — ICON
VACALIEBRES

Hiroshima mon amour

-094-

NEW RETRO — ICON
VACALIEBRES

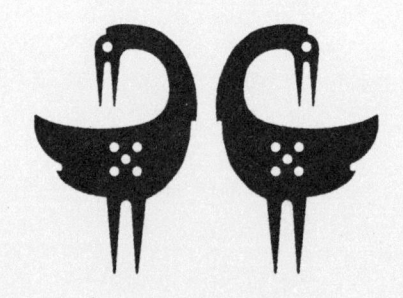

Hiroshima mon amour

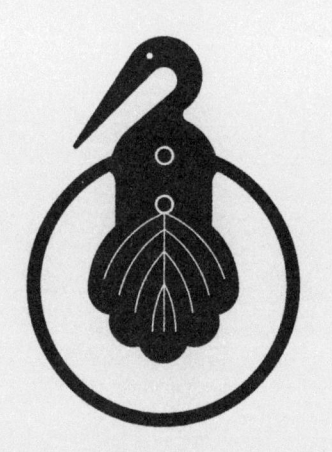

```
CD - creative direction
CL - client
CP - copywriting
CR - special credits
DE - design
IL - illustration
IN - interior design
PH - photography
PT - printing
```

✶ RETRO ✶ IN DESIGN

THIS CHAPTER IS COMPRISED OF COMPREHENSIVE GRAPHIC SOLUTIONS GARNERED FROM ESTABLISHED AND EMERGING DESIGNERS AROUND THE WORLD WHO ALL APPRECIATES BEAUTY THAT WITHSTANDS TIME. THE SELECTION EXAMINES HOW TIME-HONOURED VISUAL ELEMENTS SUCH AS PRINT FINISHES, PATTERNS, ILLUSTRATIONS, PALETTES, AND CLASSIC TYPEFACES ARE APPLIED TO ENGENDER FASHIONABLE IDENTITIES AND COMMUNICATIONS. ACCOMPANYING DESCRIPTIONS PROVIDE INSIGHT INTO DESIGNER'S INGENUITY OF STRATEGIC BRANDING EVOCATIVE OF HISTORIC AND CULTURAL CONNOTATIONS.

P. 098 ———— P. 247

BASIC STAMPS
Duane Dalton

Basic Stamps is an ongoing postage stamp project initiated by Duane Dalton. Marrying his love for design and stamps, the Irish graphic artist has created more than 80 stamp designs with a characteristic approach to turn them into a series. With simply shapes, colours and typefaces, these little art pieces identify a number of countries and organisations with their spirit and landscape.

- 099 -

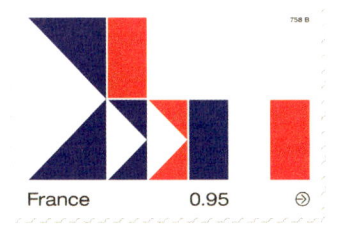

STAMPS

Ryan Chapman

CL Kokomo Coffee (P.101)

The brilliant use of soft shapes and colours is unmistakable in Ryan Chapman's illustration. Depicting aquatic life, Denmark Underwater on this page is one of his recent attempts to illustrate a country by relevant activities. On facing page is a set of stickers designed for Estonian coffee label, Kokomo Coffee. These cheery stamps form part of the brand's packaging to mark the African and South American origins of their four coffee blends in a delightful way.

40
CENT
REPUBLIQUE
40
CENT
RWANDA IKAWA
50
CENT
BAADA PEPE
50
CENT
KENYA KAHAWA
20
CENT
POSTAGE DUE
20
CENT
ETHIOPIA BUNA
30
CTS
CORREO AEREO
30
CTS
COSTA RICA CAFÉ

ØYENVITNE

Anna Kövecses

CL Øyenvitne

Appearing calm and poetic, these book cover illustrations prelude four new crime novels to be published by Øyenvitne, a Norwegian publishing house whose name translates as "eyewitness". The graphic approach contrasts the usual dark covers that induce a mysterious setting, and intrigues readers in a way that matches the young Scandinavian authors' styles. A logo with a peering face was also conceived, that animates on the publisher's folded business cards.

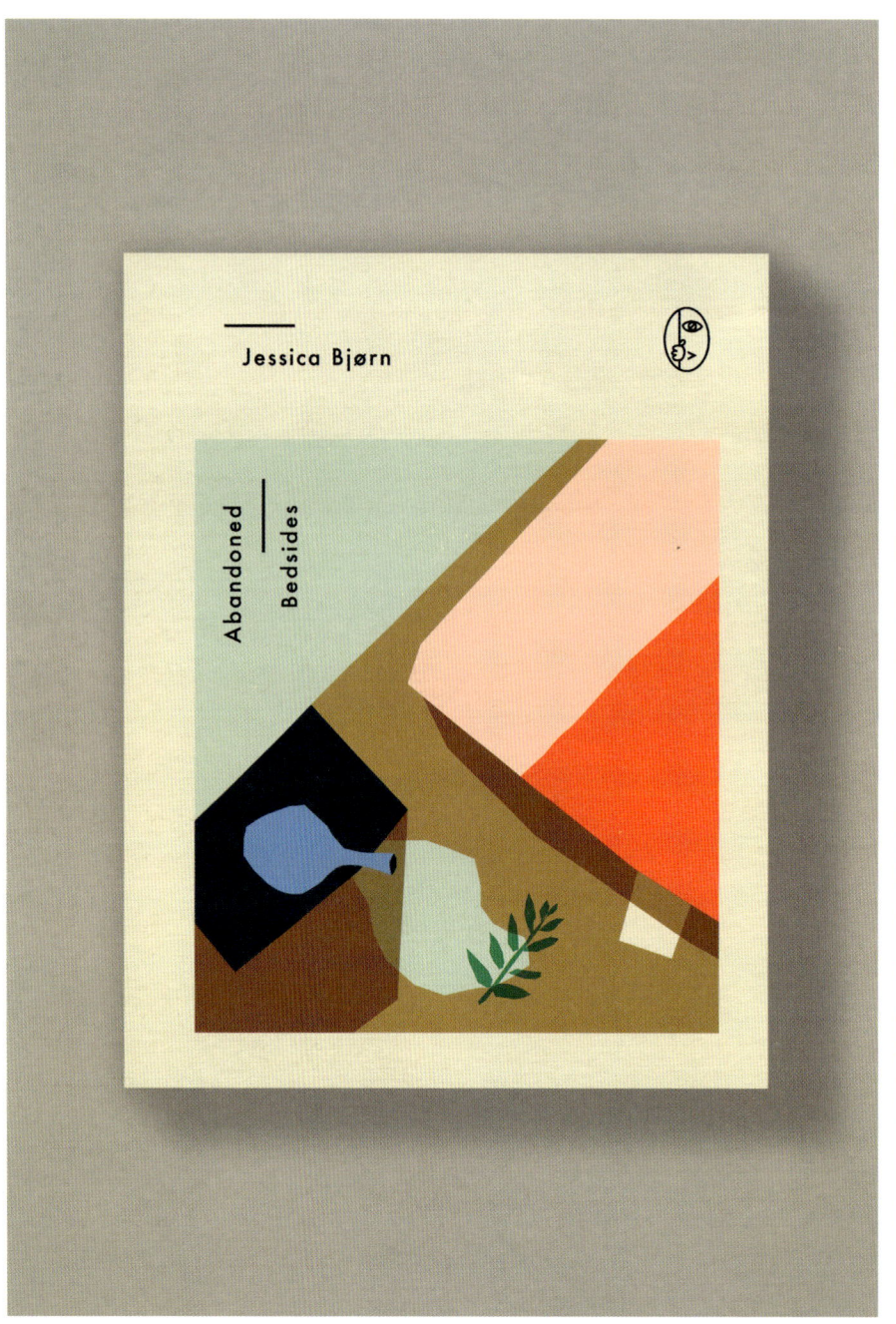

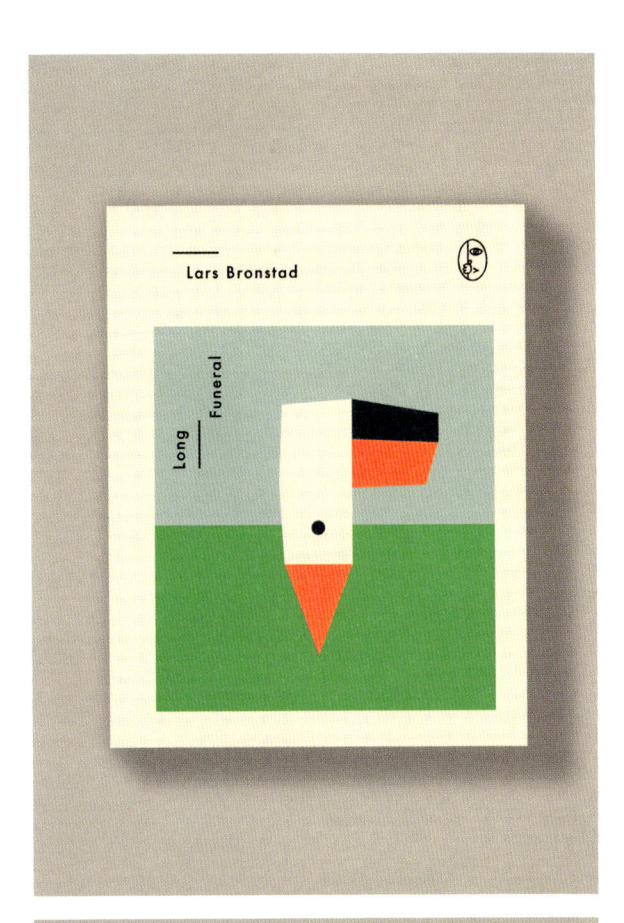

Lars Bronstad

Long Funeral

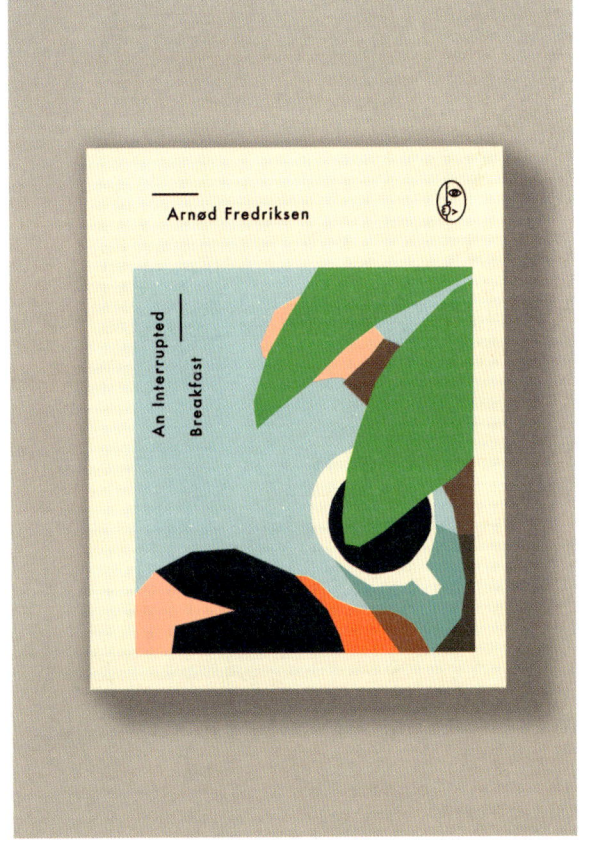

Arnød Fredriksen

An Interrupted Breakfast

NEW FRONTIERS

atelier bingo.

```
CL New Frontiers
```

Organised by MA Publishing students at London College of Communication, the 11th Publishing Innovation Conference focused on how stories are told in the media today. Seemingly random elements dance around the event's poster to denote an eclectic programme featuring star speakers involved in various aspects of the current reading culture. Curators, social media specialists, publishers, writers and journalists could all be found in the line-up.

BIOGRAFIAS VIMARANENSES

Non-Verbal Club

PT Margarida Castel-Branco
CL Guimarães 2012 European Capital of Culture

Biografias Vimaranenses contains the life stories and achievements of 12 individuals that occurred in Portuguese city Guimarães. Celebrating individuality and the historical account, a thousand covers were uniquely produced for different copies of the book. Each comprises a varied geometry-based composition singly made by overlaying silkscreen prints, with fluorescent pink to add a contemporary touch.

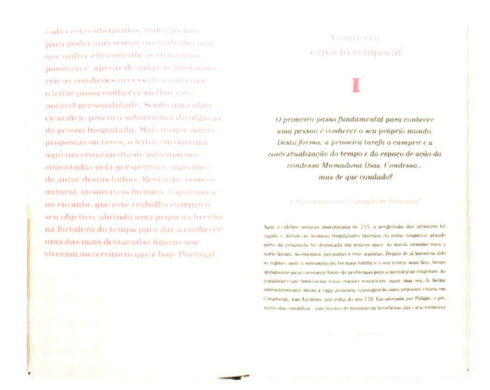

AGENDA CCCB
Hey

PH Roc Canals
CL CCCB

Centre de Cultura Contemporània de Barcelona (CCCB) publishes a programme guide every two months. Seeing the centre as a receptacle for contemporary ideas, Hey graphically interpreted the cultural centre's building in a profusion of colours and shapes for the 2013 series, that continues to illuminate the booklet's inner pages. The abstract patterns were aimed to create a lasting appeal and invite imagination.

- 107 -

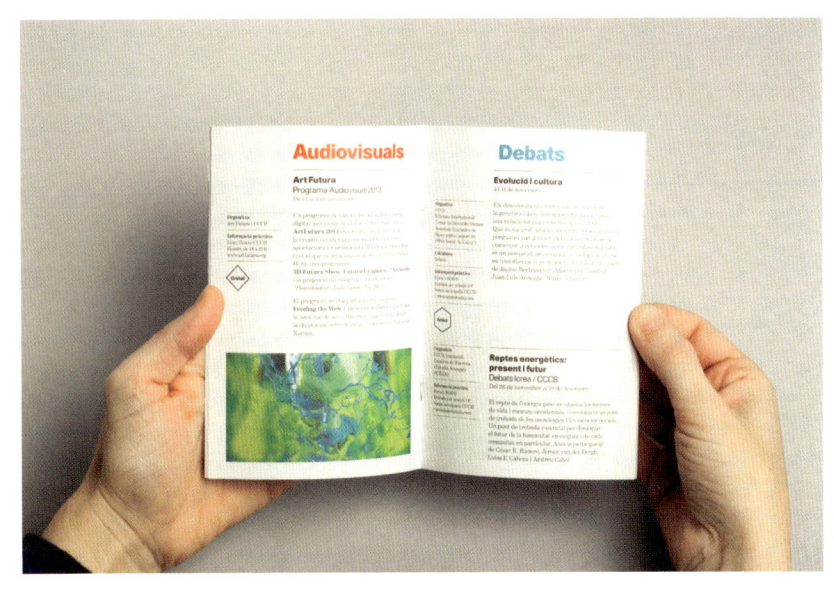

PAUL & MARIGOLD

Foreign Policy Design Group

CL Paul & Marigold

In a set of four, these miniature literature classics affirm Paul & Marigold's affinity with literary work. With a 'hard' cover featuring a gold-foiled book title and decorative lines, these books function as the boutique publishing house's business cards, which unfold the company's contact methods and story over a double-page spread inside. The details were laid out in the style of a book's content page for a complete look.

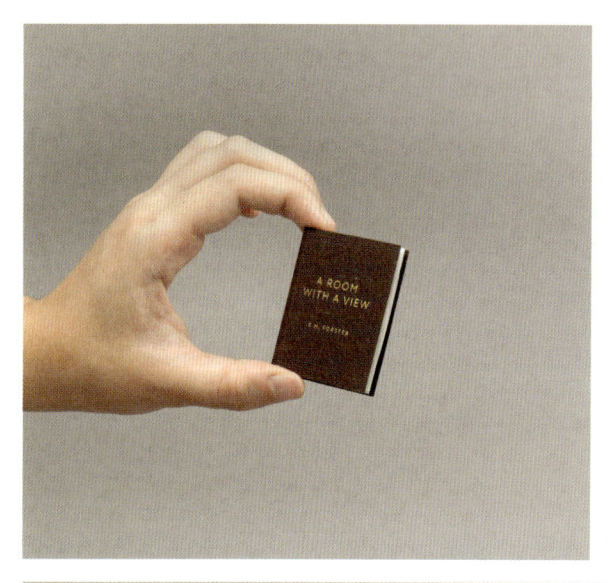

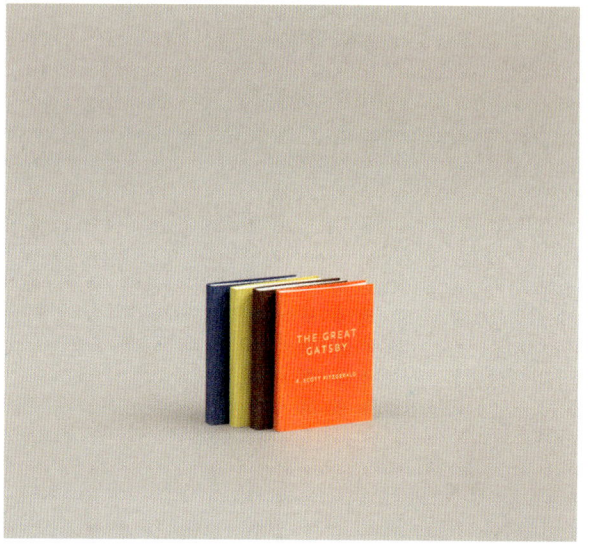

- 109 -

BRAND GUIDE: SINGAPORE EDITION
Foreign Policy Design Group

Foreign Policy has initiated a new project to document the making of 17 iconic Singaporean brands with a multidimensional, analytical approach. The first of their Brand Guide series sets the tone and format of the forthcoming guides, with a kraft paper folder holding brand materials of all sizes and shapes, organising design concepts and process into an informative portfolio that invites exploration. Completely hand-assembled, each guide accents the brand owners and designers' first-hand accounts with personal touches.

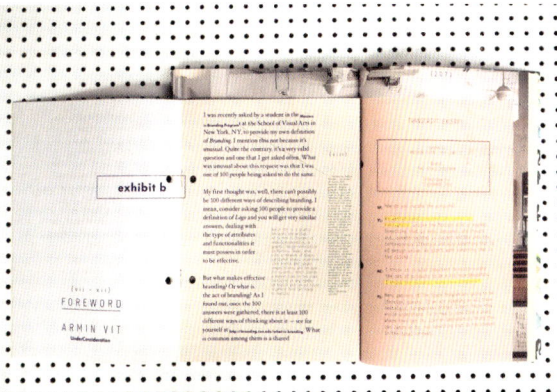

- 111 -

HISTORY OF BRANDING

Strategically located in the heart of Southeast Asia, **Singapore** in its early days attracted strings of immigrants across multiple backgrounds arriving in search of new beginnings. Over the years, this cu...

BRAND
REPORT
(N°2)

The Lo & Behold Group

Wander lust Hotel

Loosely adapted from the German language, Wanderlust describes a desire to explore new and foreign places in search of an escape or new discoveries. Drawing from this same spirit, Wanderlust Hotel draws from its rich heritage location of Little India as an unexpected location for a hotel to reside in. ==It encourages travellers to get to know unfamiliar cultures, ways of life, and behaviours present in the ethnic== diversity of Singapore.

PLAIN VANILLA
BAKERY

MAP OF
Singapore

BRAND REPORT (N°4)

Goodstuph
Museum of Singapore
Working Capitol
DrGL
Shunmugam
Food For Thought
The Loco Group
Coffee Roasters
Plain Vanilla
BooksActually
Grafunkt
PACT
Supermama
Space Program

BRAND REPORT (N°1)
Papa Palheta

This story begins with a hero — the very man who gave this company its name — *Colonel Francisco de Melo Palheta*. In the early 1700s, the Brazilian colonel was sent to neighbouring *French Guiana* to acquire the *prized crop*, and as some stories go, the officer charmed the governor's wife into presenting him with a bouquet of flowers that contained cuttings from a *coffee plant*, which fathered the generations of Brazilian-grown coffee from that point on.

Strait of Singapore, off the 'S' tip of ...nsula.
an independent republic comprising this island and a few adjacent islets; member of the Commonwealth of Nations; formerly a British crown colony (1946–59) and member of the Federation of Malaysia (1963–65). 220 sq. mi. (570 sq. km). *Capital:* Singapore

a seaport in and the capital of this republic.

Related forms
singaporean, noun, adjective

THE WORKING CAPITOL
Foreign Policy Design Group

CL Bamboo Group

The Working Capitol is a community of knowledge workers who operate at the intersection of creativity, technology, and business. The brand concept was created based on the Euclidean principle which then inspired a visual language, introducing the shared office's goal to provide a beautiful space enhanced by contemporary lifestyle and a community support system. The different permutations of the logo system expand to reflect an intricate and infinite sphere of influence within the space, while a clean, assertive typeface connects with the intelligent minds.

- 115 -

GUIMARÃES JAZZ 2012 POSTERS

Non-Verbal Club

CL Centro Cultural Vila Flor

Going for a solution at variance with the previous year's that vibrantly celebrated Guimarães Jazz Festival's 20th birthday, Non-Verbal Club switched to highlight the musical instruments typically used to play jazz for the festival's 21st edition. Abstractions of drums, saxophones and piano keys frisking around the poster channel the spirit of the music genre, with a vintage look to tribute its golden days. A warm palette finishes off the design, transmitting the geniality that filled jazz musicians and enthusiasts from that era.

> I just look for them in a different way. I'm looking for a new way to say "I love you".
>
> *Dave Douglas*

JAZZ

GUIMARÃES JAZZ
8 A 17 — NOV — 2012
CENTRO CULTURAL VILA FLOR

QUINTA 08 HERBIE HANCOCK - PLUGGED IN. A NIGHT OF SOLO EXPLORATIONS • **SEXTA 09** BILL FRISELL / BILL MORRISON: THE GREAT FLOOD • **SÁBADO 10** DAVE DOUGLAS & JOE LOVANO QUINTET: SOUND PRINTS • **DOMINGO 11** BIG BAND E ENSEMBLE DE CORDAS DA ESMAE DIRIGIDOS POR JACAM MANRICKS • **DOMINGO 11** LUCIAN BAN ENESCO RE-IMAGINED • **QUARTA 14** JACAM MANRICKS BAND • **QUINTA 15** PROJETO TOAP/GUIMARÃES JAZZ 2012 | OJM COM MÚSICA DE JOÃO PAULO ESTEVES DA SILVA • **SEXTA 16** THE JAZZ PASSENGERS RE-UNITED • **SÁBADO 17** WDR BIG BAND COLOGNE PLAYS THE MUSIC OF RANDY BRECKER

CENTRO CULTURAL VILA FLOR
GUIMARÃES

GUIMARÃES 2012
CAPITAL EUROPEIA DA CULTURA

VINTAGE POSTERS
Mads Berg Illustration

CL Bornholm; On facing page (clockwise) Elsevier magazine, Aiglon Magazine, Air Greenland, Monocle magazine

The harmonic fusion of classic poster design and modern brand visions are hallmark features of Mads Berg's illustrations. This is evident in his work produced to promote tourism for the island of Bornholm in Denmark and the posters for Air Greenland, Elsevier (a Dutch weekly) and Swiss boarding school Aiglon's magazine. Sometimes Berg also incorporates messages into his colour scheme, such as the identity of Denmark that prevails the cover of Monocle Magazine's annual national survey.

- 119 -

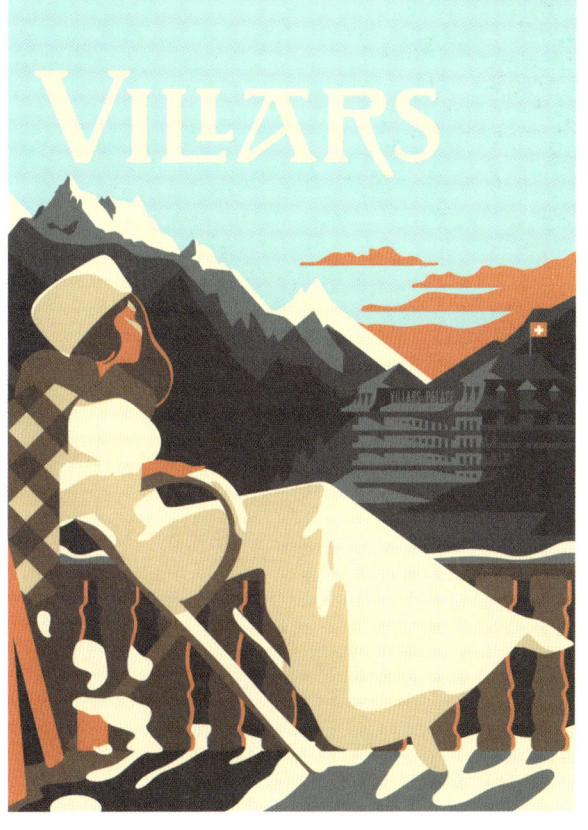

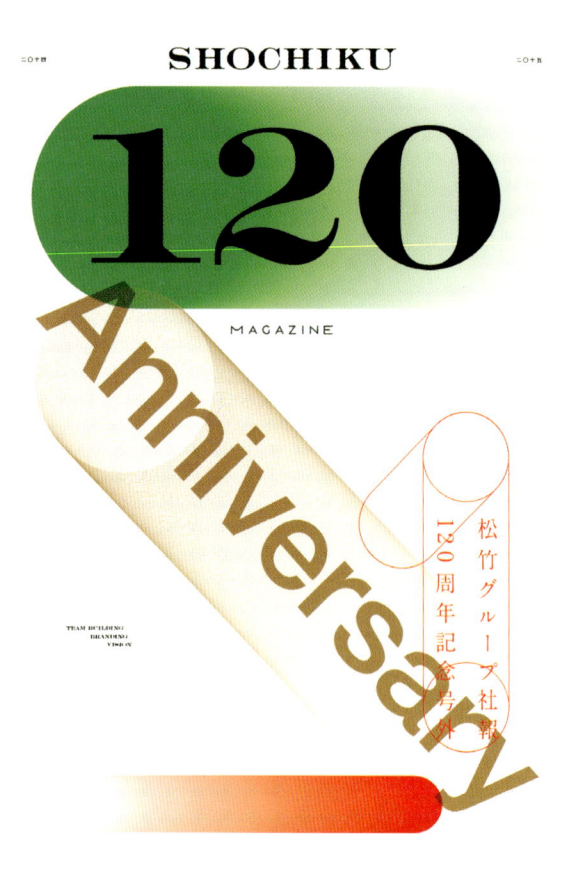

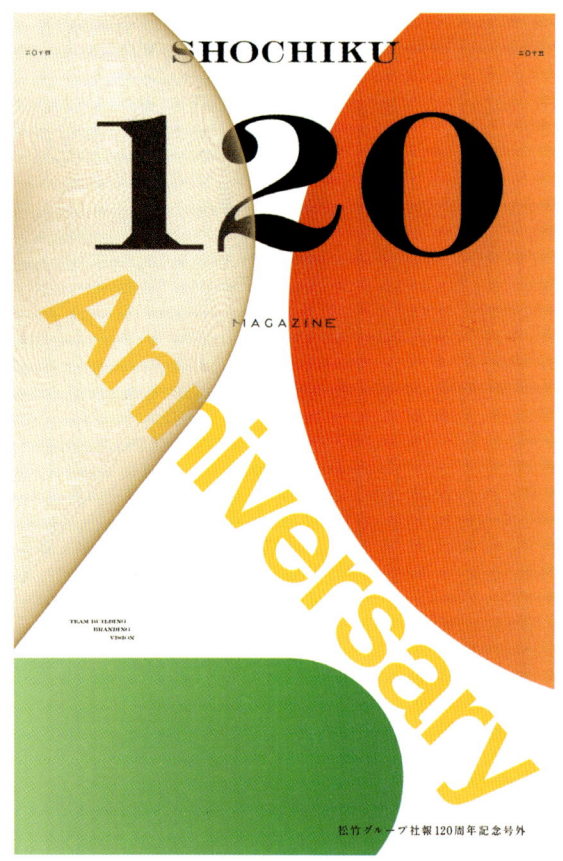

SHOCHIKU MAGAZINE 2015
Motoi Shito

CL Shochiku Co., Ltd

Shochiku's movie productions focus on Japanese dance-drama kabuki. On its 120th anniversary, the company's internal magazine published a special issue, with the number '120' played up and bleeding the cover's rims to heap praise on the company's great achievements. While colours tie glory with Shochiku and the country, a vintage tone alludes to centuries-old national art.

THISWEEK

Motoi Shito

CL THISWEEK

THISWEEK is all about great DJ music set off by visual projections. A graphic rendition of the evening event, these posters foretell its stella lineup with the name recurring as a party of tricolour blocks and slender typeface to reinforce the unique vibe. The eyes remind viewers that their programme does not only entertain their hearing but also their sights.

SPLIT STONES
Jared Bell

CL Western Vinyl

"Split Stones" originates from the idea of disparate halves coming together — a metaphor for the band and brothers' geographical divide, the dichotomy of rational thoughts and human behaviour, and the organic components derived from electronic music. Noting a vague resemblance to what Surrealist and Metaphysical art manifest, Jared Bell, as one half of the band, explored the curious relationships in a similarly symbolic way.

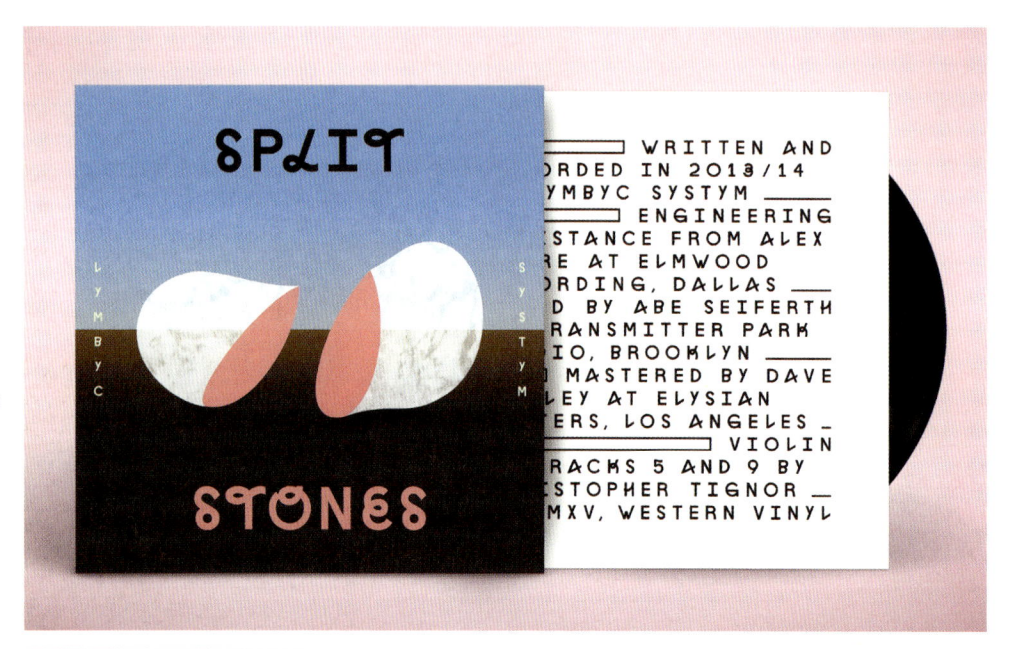

DIMMING AWE, THE LIGHT IS RAW

Jared Bell

CL Western Vinyl

Under the Botany moniker, artist and producer Spencer Stephenson creates danceable and rich psychological tunes. For his second album, *Dimming Awe, The Light is Raw*, Jared Bell interpreted the experimental drone, weaving together geographical abstractions referencing the art of Bauhaus masters Anni Albers and Laszlo Moholy-Nagy alike. The result is a 12-inch vinyl LP packaging with a removable J-card style spine cover that unfolds into a poster.

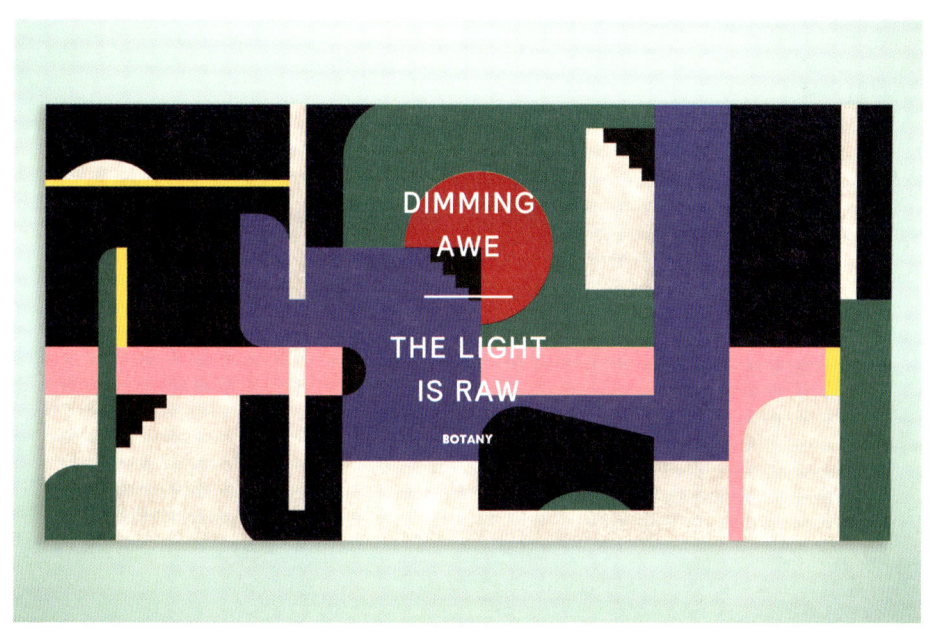

TRANSIENT SENSES
Pol Pintó Fabregat

CR EINA, Centre Universitari de Disseny i Art de Barcelona

A site-specific installation created for Sónar+D, a conference about creativity and technology, Transient Senses by artist Alex Arteaga investigates Mies van der Rohe Pavilion's open-plan design with visuals, textual and sound. The ephemeral nature of these elements was graphically conveyed on the event's collateral, resulting in a dynamic reflection not to be forgotten.

Transient Senses
Alex Arteaga
Pavelló Mies Van der Rohe
07.04.2015 | 10.05.2015
Transient Senses
Alex Arteaga
Pavelló Mies Van der Rohe
07.04.2015 | 10.05.2015
Transient Senses
Alex Arteaga
Pavelló Mies Van der Rohe
07.04.2015 | 10.05.2015
Transient Senses
Alex Arteaga
Pavelló Mies Van der Rohe
07.04.2015 | 10.05.2015
Transient Senses
Alex Arteaga
Pavelló Mies Van der Rohe
07.04.2015 | 10.05.2015

Transient Senses
Alex Arteaga
Pavelló Mies Van der Rohe
07.04.2015 | 10.05.2015
Transient Senses
Alex Arteaga
Pavelló Mies Van der Rohe
07.04.2015 | 10.05.2015

DHUB
Lo Siento

CL DHUB

A set of handouts was produced to promote the opening of Design Museum of Barcelona (DHUB) in 2014. Images of the museum building, collections and text compliment each other in a contrasting tones. All leaflets were produced in poster format, with three fluorescent hues to set apart the different language editions and scream for attention.

Museu del Disseny de Barcelona
VISITAS GUIADAS

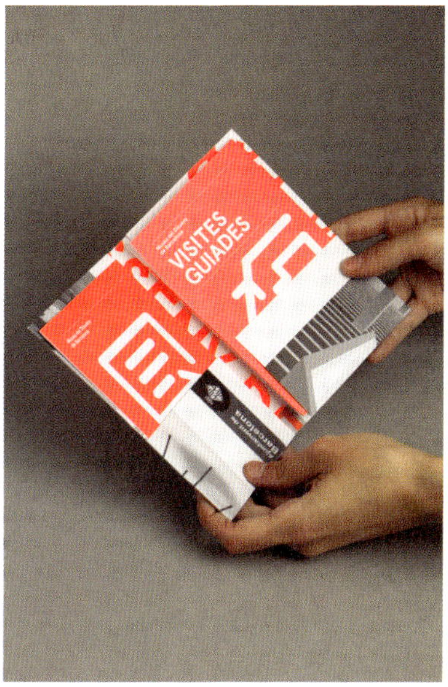
VISITES GUIADES

AQUESTA ÉS LA SEU DEL NOU MUSEU DEL DISSENY DE BARCELONA
Ajuntament de Barcelona
bcn.cat/museudeldisseny
Recerca
Documentació
Conservació
Restauració
Difusió
Innovació
Coneixement
MÉS DE 70.000 OBJECTES
Està previst obrir les portes del museu al públic la primavera del 2014
Exposicions
Centre de Documentació
Tallers
Conferències
Serveis educatius
Experimentació
Serveis en línia
Publicacions
Visites guiades
RECERCA I DIFUSIÓ DEL DISSENY

ST JAMES'S LONDON LOCAL AREA GUIDES

dn&co.

IL Katie Scott
PT Push Print
CL The Crown Estate

As part of a placemaking project on St James's, a historic district in central London, four visitor guides were compiled to bring to light the area's core but underrated strengths in food, fashion and art, alongside an everyday amenities guide for local workers. Easy and attractive to read, the guides aim to right out-of-date views with up-to-date reviews and beautiful illustrations. The set is up for grabs at retailers and cultural institutions, each in a characteristic brand colour.

- 129 -

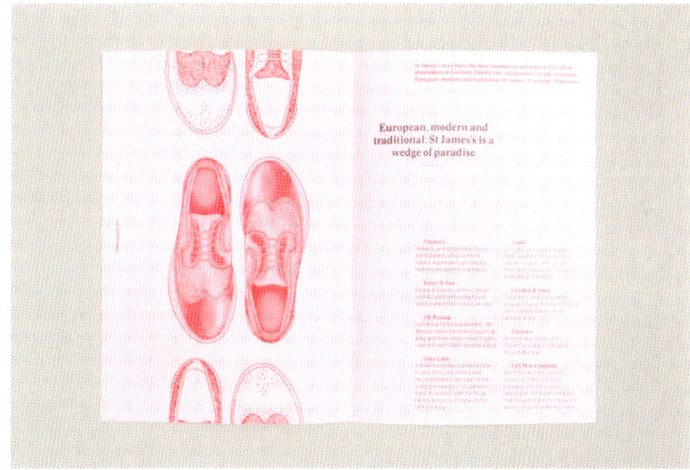

DELICIOUS POSTCARDS
Joe Haddad

PH Darrin Haddad Photography

Sharing is caring — that's why Joe Haddad created Delicious Postcards to log and share the joy of munching a hot sandwich at a classic eatery in New York City on a cold, snowy day. To complete his graphic memory of what he ate and he loves about New York snacks, a rounded plastic type common on special meal boards behind the cashier counters was used to name the item or ingredients on the card's back.

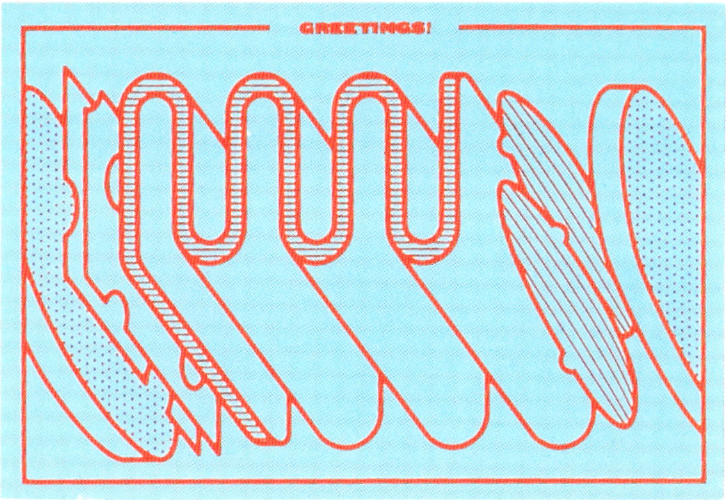
GREETINGS!

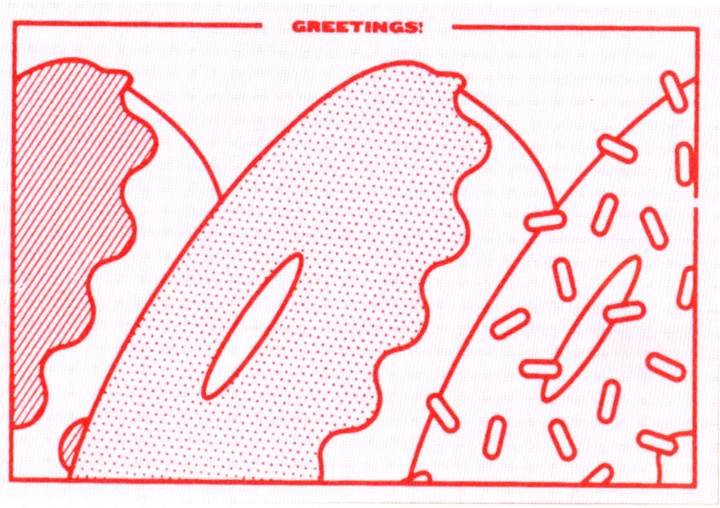
GREETINGS!

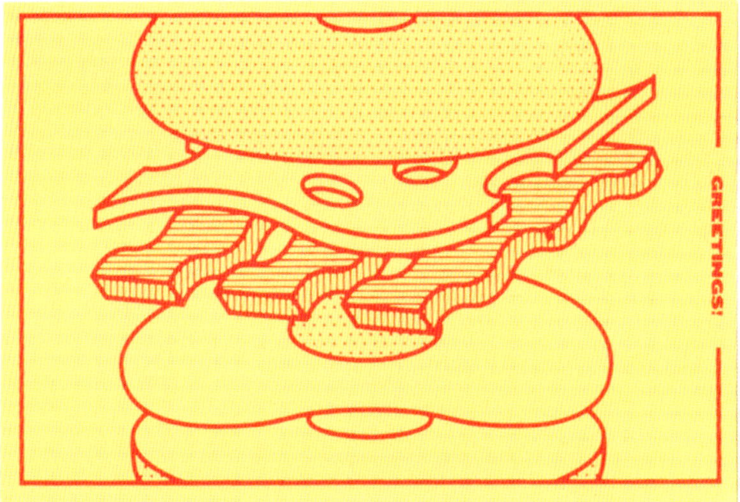
GREETINGS!

RISOGRAPH PRINTING CALENDAR 2015

O.OO Risograph Printing & Design ROOM

In an edition of 200, the six-page calendar has come as the result of Risograph printing experimentation. Using seven colour ink, the stencil duplication process created subtle nuances of lines, shapes and colour layers, leading to absolutely unique designs on every print. Perforated lines made for a thoughtful addition, allowing users to tear off the colourful prints for collection after every two months.

- 133 -

UNFINISHED DAYDREAM
O.OO Risograph Printing & Design ROOM

Playing with visual texture, colours, shapes and line patterns, Unfinished Daydream was carried out to manifest the potential of Risograph printing. With colours limited to orange, blue and green, these illustrations reveal interesting interactions between colour patches and graphic elements of various volume and densities. The prints were produced in poster and postcard formats for enjoyment.

- 135 -

CIRCA

Bunker3022

PH Magali Seberian
CL Circa

Circa specialises in fabric print design. To demonstrate their commitment to bringing joy through their bold, beautiful prints, the Argentine company's brand identity unifies these elements into a coherent and communicative language, through a collage of archive images, modern patterns and Circa's hallmark prints. A warm palette reinforces the idea across its business cards and packaging bags.

- 137 -

KIXBOX SS14 SAMPLE SALE
Facultative Works

CL Kixbox

Whether these illustrations depicted a real or fictional post-apocalyptic scene, Kixbox will let Russia's cool crowd find out at its multi-label boutiques. Made to announce the store's limited-time sample sale, these images winnow out the cliché marketing tag lines and intrigue viewers by imagining what would happen as nuclear winter arrives. Every street wear item help reveal a corner of an emptied flat and an episode of the story.

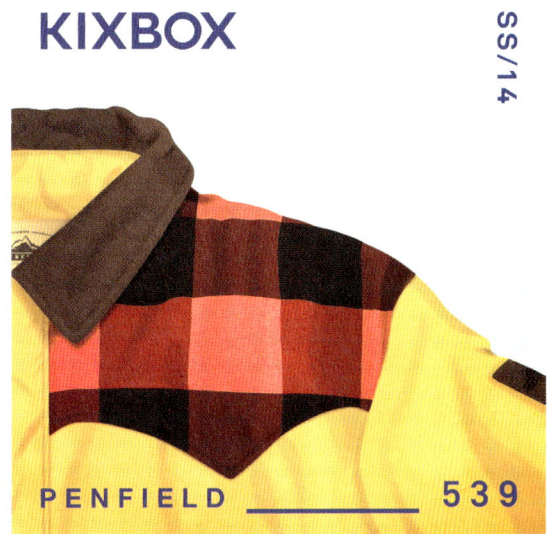

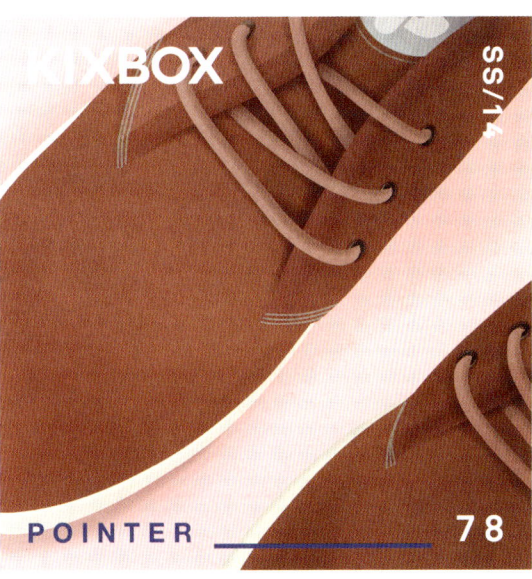

KIXBOX SS/14 ГОЛОВНЫЕ УБОРЫ —— 269	**KIXBOX** SS/14 PENFIELD —— 539
KIXBOX SS/14 UNDFTD —— 67	**KIXBOX** SS/14 ПОЛО —— 449
KIXBOX SS/14 ПЛАТЬЯ —— 53	**KIXBOX** SS/14 POINTER —— 78

SÉRIGRAPHIE ULDRY
COMPLIMENT CARDS

A3 Studio

PT,CL Sérigraphie Uldry

A3 Studio designed a set of A5-size
complimentary cards for Swiss silkscreen
printer, Sérigraphie Uldry. A nod to the
printer's expertise, a silk screen squeegee
dominates the card with the printer's name
recurring in the background. Only three
coloured inks were employed and a number of
variants was brought about for use.

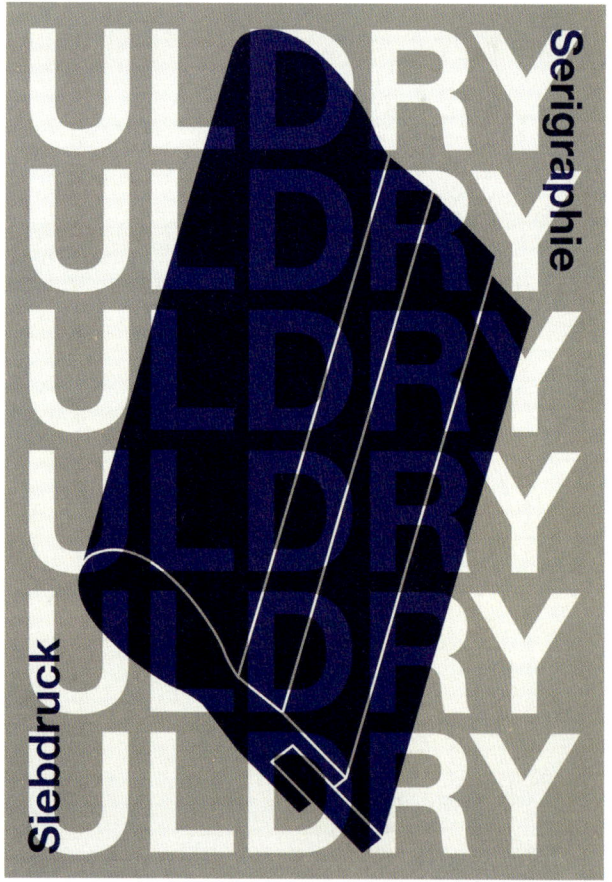

TIMELESS, MASSIMO VIGNELLI

A3 Studio

CL Husmee

"Timeless, Massimo Vignelli" is a collective exhibition that celebrates designer Massimo Vignelli's aesthetic influences on modern life. A3 Studio is among the 30 some units invited to create a graphic tribute to the late master. The result is a potpourri of iconic logos created by Vignelli, that strips down to their pure coloured shapes in absence of names and words. These shapes feature logos of the American Airlines, Benetton, Cinzano, Bloomingdales and New York subway's signage system.

B*THERE FESTIVAL 2014

Studio Daad, Studio Turbo

CL B*THERE Festival

B*THERE is an annual two-day festival of art, music and culture that takes place in Dutch city, 's-Hertogenbosch. Keen on drawing the public's immediate attention to what was about to unfold during the event, the designers drew on the warning sign language typical of the ones used in a construction sits. The raw sticks and hand-painted finishing gave off a edgy DIY feel across the posters, flyers, invitations and many more.

25 OKTOBER PROGRAM
24 OKTOBER PROGRAM
24 + 25 OKTOBER PROGRAM

24 & 25 OKTOBER 2014
SAVE THE DATE
B*THERE FESTIVAL
PARADE, DEN BOSCH

B*THERE
MEGGY ALTHUIZEN
COMMUNICATIE
WWW.B-THERE.NL

PAPA PALHETA BRAND EXPERIENCE KIT

Foreign Policy Design Group

CL Papa Palheta

The Papa Palheta experience kit is designed to engage customers in coffee culture and manifest the specialty coffee brand's strong coffee roots down to sustainability. Apart from a bag for redeeming bean samples, the kit consists of a set of cards — one made from disposed coffee chaff to encourage repurposing, a coffee tasting note, a brewing guide and a cake recipe for pairing. Geometric shapes, fluorescent colours and assorted paper stock generate a sensory experience that transcends the common brown coffee packaging.

TASTE
NOTES
& HAVE YOUR CAKE TOO
PAPAPALHETA.COM
THE GOLDEN RATIO
COFFEE
WATER
PAPA PALHETA
PAPAPALHETA.COM

- 146 -

- 147 -

HUNGARIAN INVENTORS SERIES
Absoloot

CD,DE,IL Eszter Csontos
PH Nóra Puskás, Bertalan Bessenyey
CL Magma Gallery, Budapest

Commissioned by Magma Gallery, Hungarian Inventors is an exhibition memorabilia made to commemorate the late Hungarian originators who had contribute incredible improvements to modern life. Simple to the eye but impressive by touch, the colourless Hungarian folk art motifs on the packaging box connote how their invention of ballpoint pens and refrigerators appears to the world today. Illustrated portraits and handwritings hint at the epoch where these products came to life.

- 149 -

KILL BABY KILL

studiowmw

PH Missbean
CL röyksopp gakkai

Drawing inspirations from horror films in the 1970s and 1980s and classical European children clothing as the brand's signature, röyksopp gakkai's 2015 Fall/Winter collection's theme is "a nightmare dressed like a daydream". Enveloped in a sleeve with a die-cut window, the mailers feature styling shots that aim to provoke an eerie atmosphere as if one is looking out of a window in a haunted mansion.

KILL BABY KILL

THEY STOOD AGAINST THE BOARDED WINDOW

KILL BABY KILL

COMPLETE THE SKETCH OF BROKEN PIECES

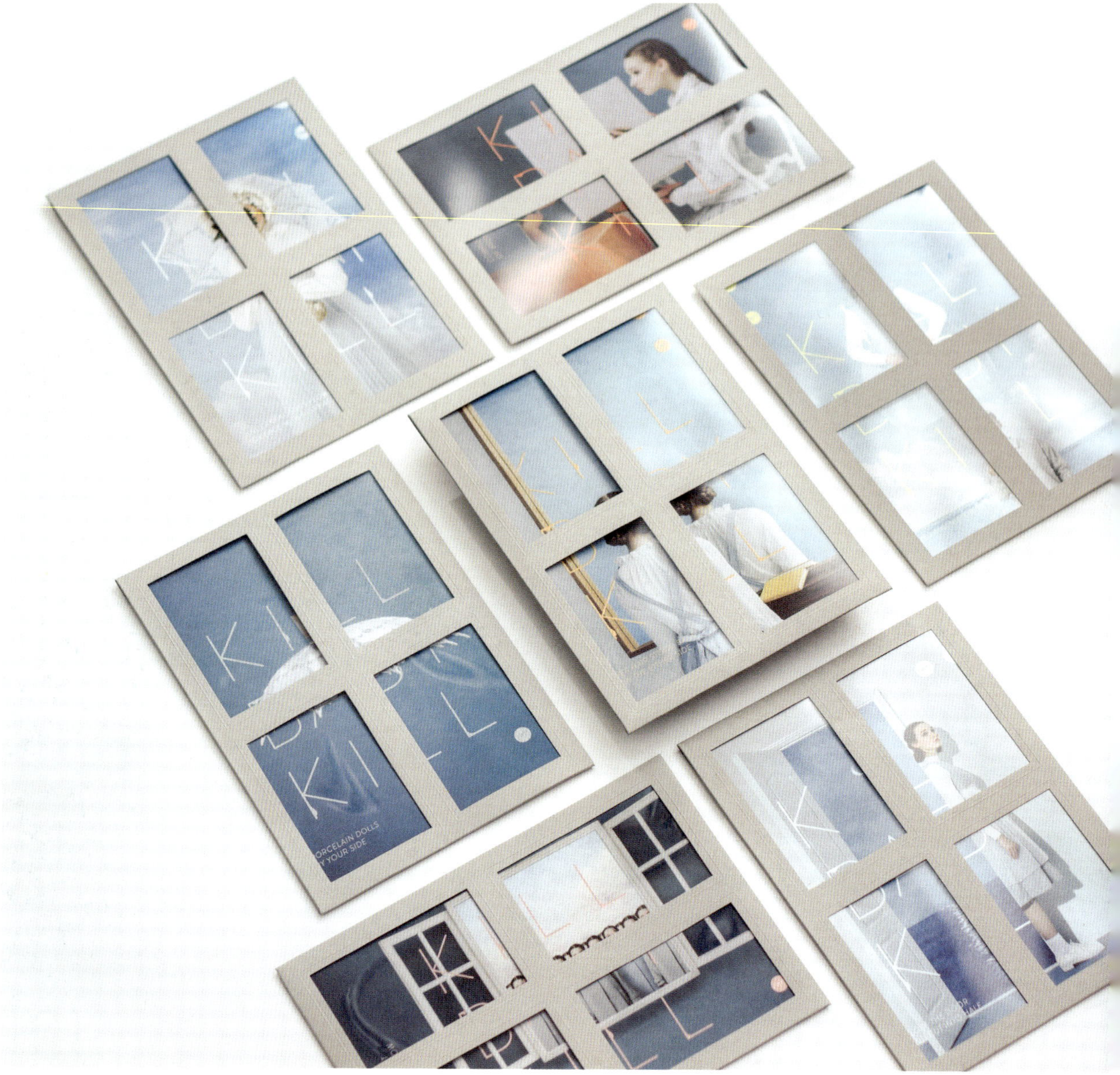

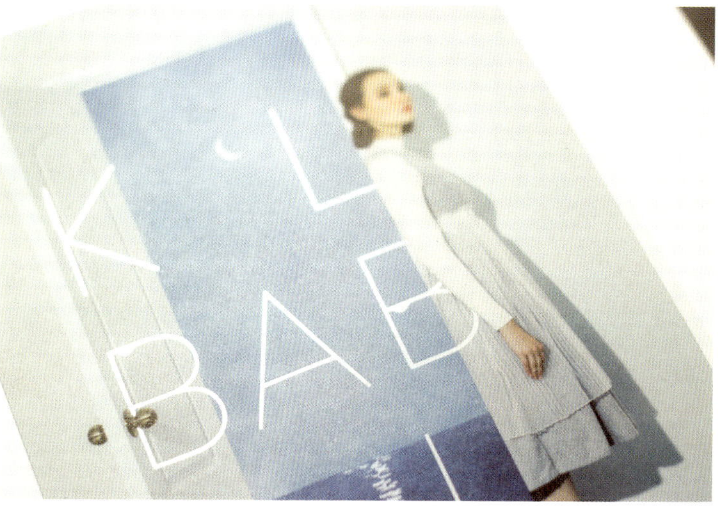

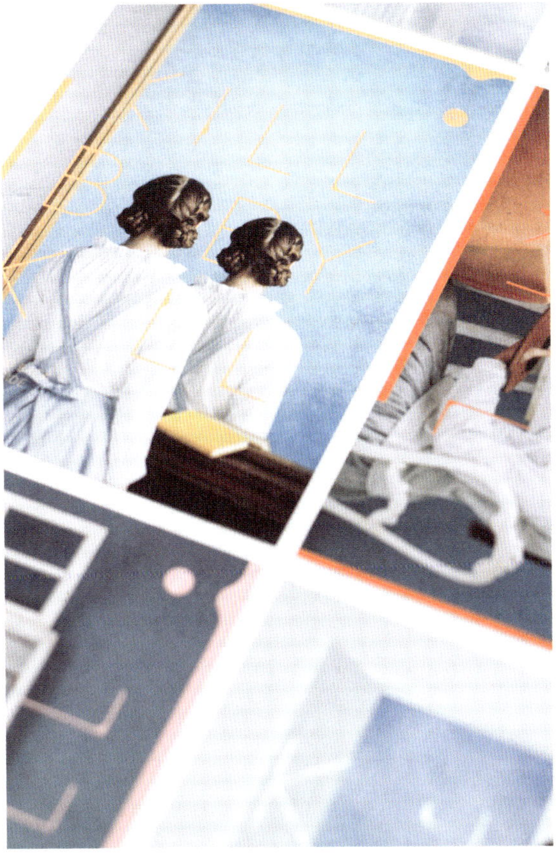

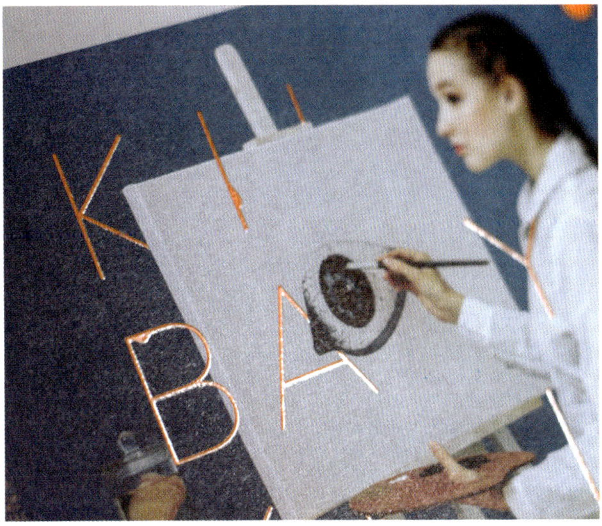

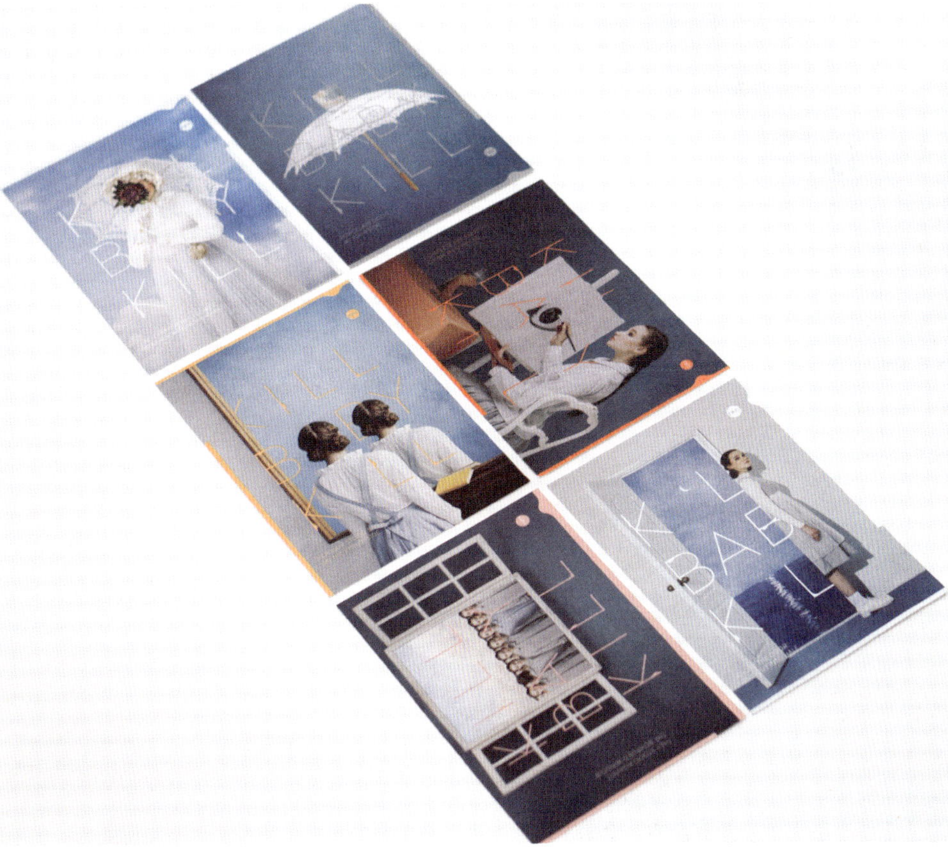

FFF-ACCURATE TOOL

Fundamental-Studio

CL Overlab

FFF is short for "form follows function", the design principle that underlies Fundamental Studio's work. Coming about as the first collaboration between Fundamental and letterpress printer, Overlab, the postcard manifests the key design approach and Overlab's superb techniques by analogy with a vernier calliper. The printer materialised the idea tangibly by print.

20
FUNDAMENTAL
Refining Extraordinary Design
13
3
FASHION
FUNCTION
FUNDAMENTAL
REFINING
idea
FUNDAMENTAL
F
INSPIRATION
REAL
Beauty
BEARS
FUNCTIONS
F3
F
FFF
EXPLORE
future classic
We do premium visual communication
that enhances corporate identity
Print & Web design
• FUNDAMENTAL-STUDIO.COM
FOLLOW
FORM
FUNCTION
FFF
FUNDAMENTAL
STUDIO·FUNDAMENTAL
FORM FOLLOW FUNCTION
FUNDAMENTAL
F·F·F
INSPIRATION
FOR ALL
FORM FOLLOW FUNCTION
ACCURATE
TOOL
20
13

COCOA COLONY
Bravo

CL KOP

The brand Cocoa Colony is inspired by the brothers who brought cocoa beans from Colonial Ecuador to Europe. Tracing the long forgotten benefits of consuming cocoa beans, Cocoa Colony's graphic identity uses enormous gold elements to hark back to a time when the beans were referred to as "Amazonian Gold" for its healing properties. The typographic choice and the materiality of its brand elements both play a part in retelling the story.

COCOA COLONY
COOKIES & CREAM

COCOA COLONY

REPUBLIC OF ECUADOR
COCOA COLONY

COCOA COLONY

COCOA COLONY

REPUBLIC OF ECUADOR

COCOA COLONY
CHOCOLATE BAR

SEA SALT
MILK CHOCOLATE BAR

AMAZONIAN GOLD
heirloom variety
PREMIUM QUALITY COCOA
110g

PEANUT BUTTER
MILK CHOCOLATE

PEANUT BUTTER
MILK CHOCOLATE BAR
AMAZONIAN GOLD
PREMIUM QUALITY COCOA
110g
REPUBLIC OF ECUADOR
COCOA COLONY
ALMOND
MILK CHOCOLATE BAR
AMAZONIAN GOLD
PREMIUM QUALITY COCOA
110g

CAPPAN STUDIO

Zealplus

CL CAPPAN STUDIO

Branding for printer CAPPAN STUDIO salutes letterpress as a traditional printing technique which they strive to perfect with recourse to the latest technology. Typography is integral to CAPPAN's logo and visual identity design, denoting their adherence to printing with movable types. Juxtaposing classic typefaces with a modified letter 'C', ZEALPLUS ensured the idea of tradition and modernity play equal parts in the brand.

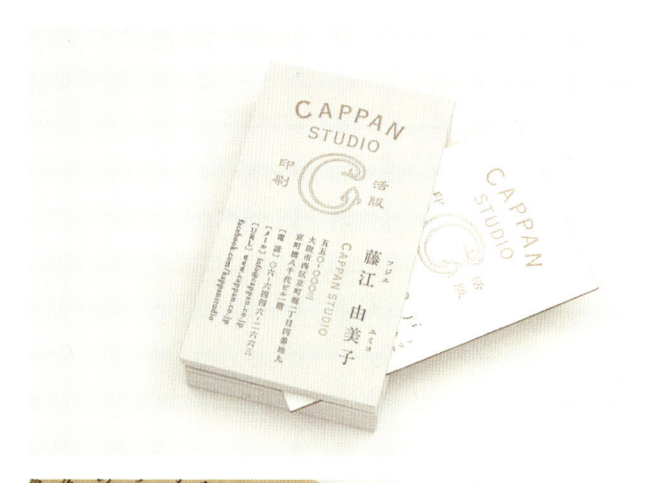

STUDIO
CAPPAN
KYOMACHIBASHI YACHIYO BLDG., 1-4-9 KYOMACHIBORI,NISHI-KU, OSAKA-CITY, 550-0003 JAPAN
WWW.CAPPAN.CO.JP

RECEIPT
NO.
DATE
DESCRIPTION
¥
CAPPAN STUDIO
TEL
NAME
DESCRIPTION
06 6446 2663
URL
DATE
CAPPAN
STUDIO
THIS IS AN OFFICIAL RECEIPT FOR INCOME TAX PURPOSES | RECEIPT
CAPPAN
STUDIO
KYOMACHIBASHI YACHIYO BLDG., 1-4-9 KYOMACHIBORI,NISHI-KU, OSAKA-CITY, 550-0003 JAPAN
WWW.CAPPAN.CO.JP

FOE

Oddds

CL Penguin Books

Oddds was asked to design the cover of *Foe (1986)* by J.M. Coetzee. To be published by Penguin Books as part of the 'Penguin Essentials', the cult classic was part of the satirical retelling of Robinson Crusoe, a historical fiction woven around the mariner's strange adventures. The final design was produced in the fashion of a vintage navigation map, picturing mutiny, voyage and death that centre the fiction's plot.

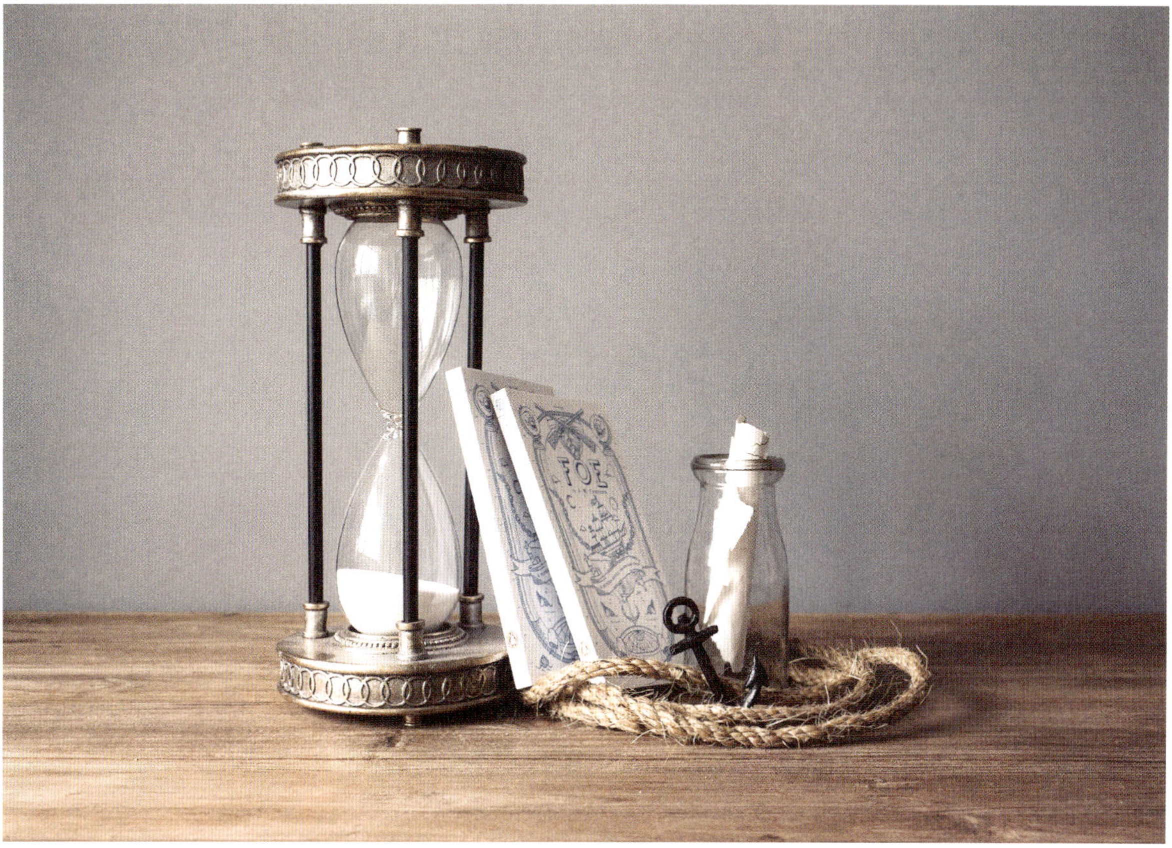
FOE

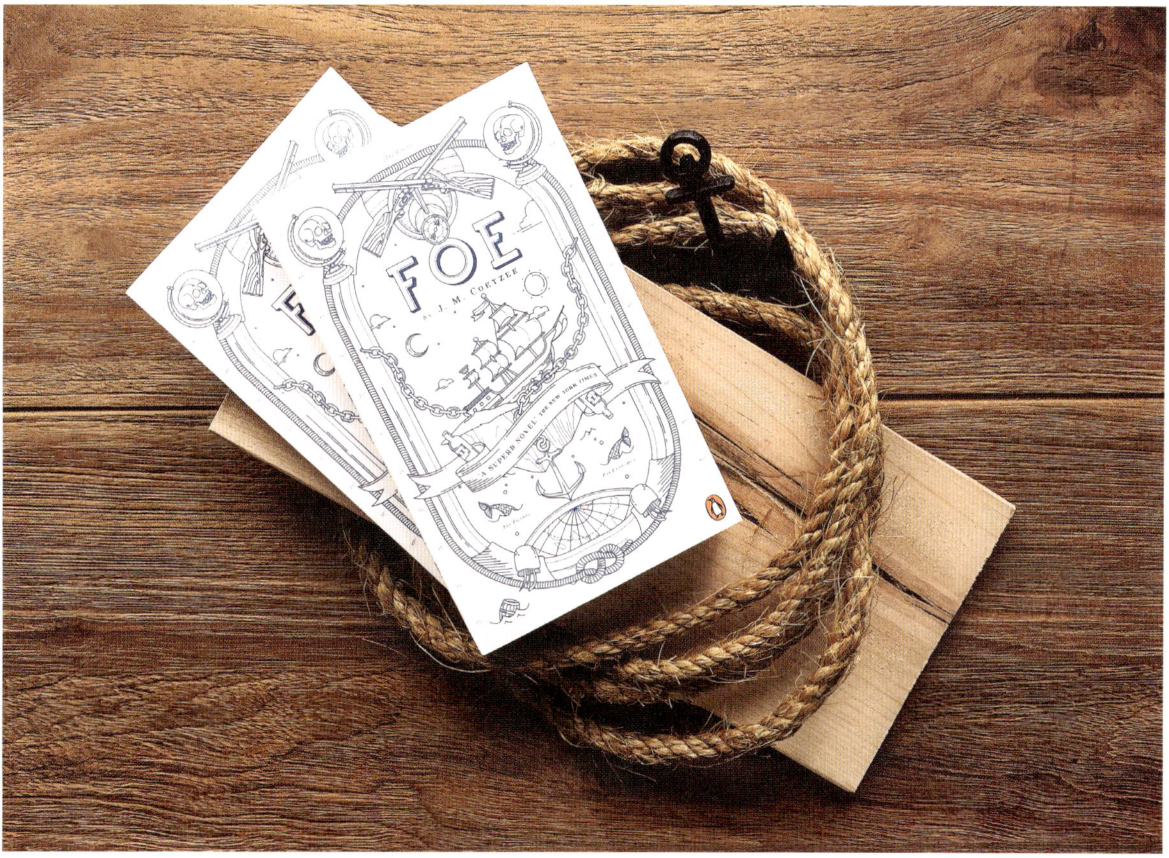
FOE
BY J. M. COETZEE

FOOD MENU
WINE LIST
DRINKS & DESSERTS
_LC_H_L
_R_NK_ &
D_SS__T_
Melissa Kowara
Managing Director

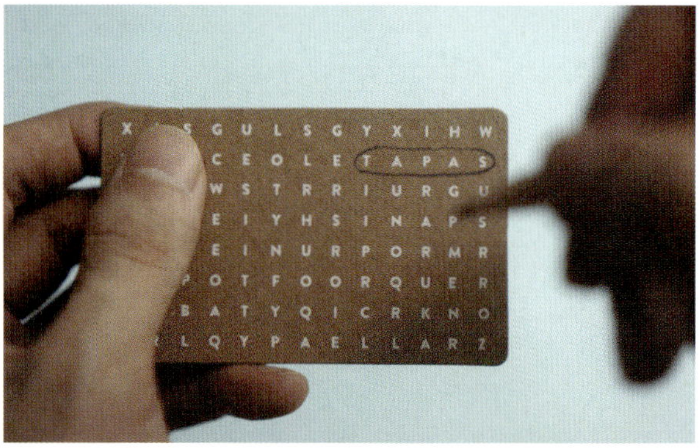

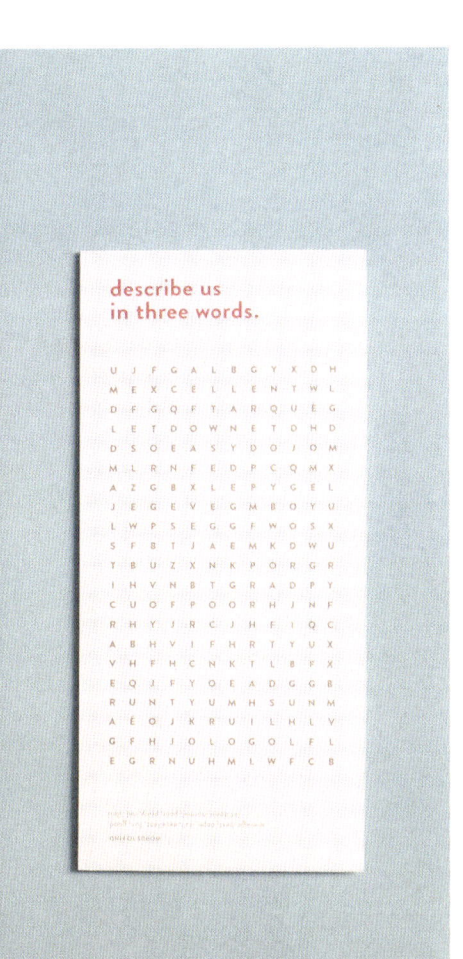

¿POR QUÉ NO?
Table Six

CL ¿Por Qué No?

¿Por Qué No? is a Spanish restaurant in Jakarta committed to topping off their tapas dishes with glee. Brand applications embrace the spirit throughout, with formats and graphics all incorporating the idea of "games". Mostly old-time games, such as crosswords and puzzles, in colours comprised of natural materials and a passionate red, the designs connect dining experience at ¿Por Qué No? with the typical Spanish hospitality and authentic tastes which the restaurant lays stress on.

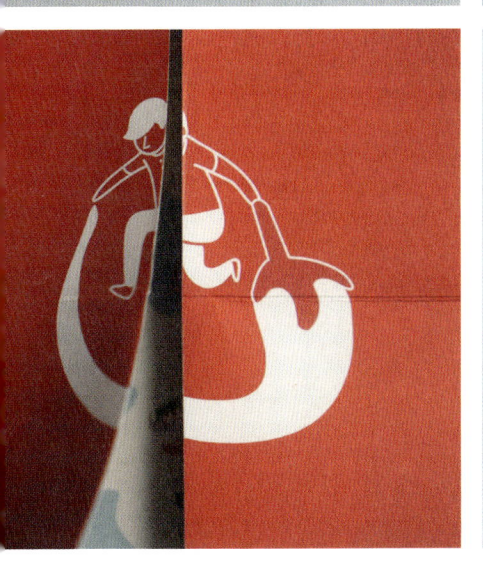

SCOUTING UNIT

Table Six

CL Scouting Unit

Scouting Unit sells daily goods that come as a collaboration between design house Table Six and selected artists, designers and manufacturers. Translating an approach that roots deep in functionality and beauty, Scouting Unit's identity positions the online store as a blank canvas where future products to perform their goodness. Muted colours and a pared-down design reiterates these values as well as confidence in their aesthetic judgement.

- 167 -

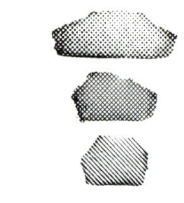

Think "Bitter"   Think "Sweet"

お菓子の仕掛け方

H.C.CREATION INITIATION CATALOGUE

UMA/design farm

CP Paradox creative Inc.
PH Yoshiro Masuda
CL H.C.Création Co., Ltd.

Three perfectly baked financiers and a delicate brand book vividly present Japanese patisserie, H.C.Creation's dedication to their potential employees. Where colourful pictures and text detail their manufacturing approach and philosophies, a gold-foiled mark repeats on the kit, bringing their baking process and a sense of quality to the fore. The line "Think 'bitter' think 'sweet'" is added to prompt young job seekers to view the cakes with a business mind.

A-CREIXEMENT

Pol Pintó Fabregat

CR EINA, Centre Universitari de Disseny i Art de Barcelona

Pol Pintó Fabregat has made a critical comment on today's consumer capitalism as his graduation project at EINA, University School of Design and Art. Titled "A-creixement", which translates as A-growth, and featuring a reversion motif, the campaign quietly calls for an insurrection and slams visual-based marketing techniques with a typographic approach. To help spread the message, a rubber stamp makes it easy to transform any mediums into effective campaign materials.

-valuar
-structurar
-distribuir
-localitzar
-duir
-utilitzar
-ciclar
-conceptualitzar
Re-

Què és l'a-creixement?
Eina
Aula 6
11.15 h
Què és l'a-creixement?
Eina
Aula 6
11.15 h
Què és l'a-creixement?
Eina
Aula 6
11.15 h
Què és l'a-creixement?
Eina
Aula 6
11.15 h

- 172 -

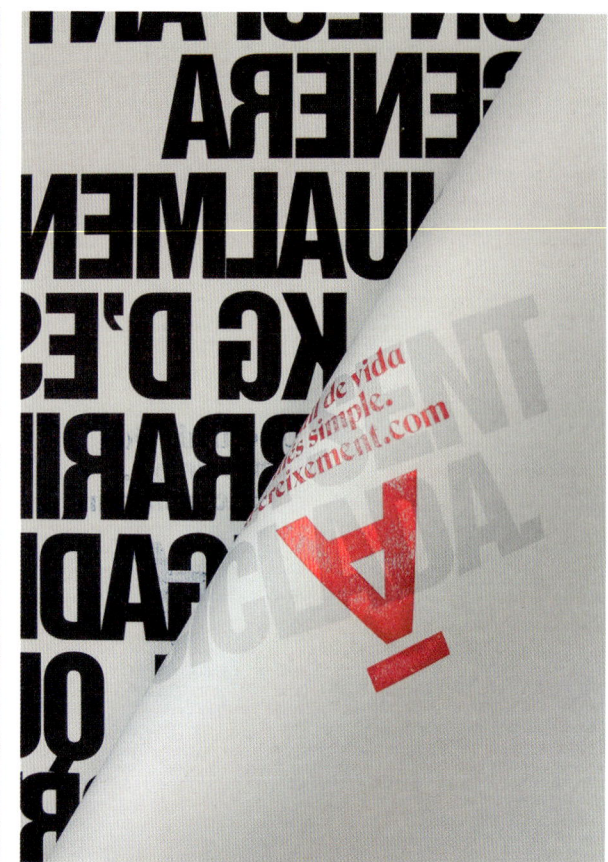

- 173 -

GOOD OLD DAYS

O.OO Risograph Printing & Design ROOM

PH Chang Chieh

Good Old Days honours letter writing and the beauty of Risograph prints. A cue for people to pick up a pen and write, retro graphics were applied to quality letter paper and the packaging box, bringing to mind a sense of sophistication and the grace of writing the age-old practice stands for. Decked with gold printing, each letter writing box contains six sets of letter sheets and envelopes alongside a complimentary postcard.

Good Old Days

Good Old Days
Good Old Days

MADE BY odot00

Good Old Days
RISOGRAPH PRINTING
STATIONERY
METALLIC GOLD
BLUE & GREEN

PORTES OUVERTES DE LA CITÉ 2014

A3 Studio

CL Portes ouvertes de la Cité

Every December, the city of Lausanne hosts Portes ouvertes de la Cité to engage the public to rediscover the charm of La Cité, an old part of town. A graphical interpretation of the event's programmes, open doors intermingle with the area's name, transmitting a sense of movement and dynamism. The varied door designs suggest the diversity of shops and museums participating in the event. A colour scheme made of blue, gold and white corresponds to the festive season.

KISSTHEDESIGN INVITATION
A3 Studio

CL Kissthedesign Gallery

Kissthedesign Gallery's fifth anniversary party was all about celebrating the number "5". The number becomes a graphic and numeral leitmotif in the party invitation design, with the message broken into five rows of five letters, spreading evenly over a pattern made of 5s. The gallery made its presence felt on the card in its corporate colour, black and pink.

JOURNÉES DES ALTERNATIVES URBAINES 2015

A3 Studio

CL Journées des alternatives urbaines

"Les Journées des alternatives urbaines" seeks to make creative ideas and experiment activities around social innovation and development visible in the city. The theme of its year 2015 edition was "Do It Together". Laying stress on a concerted effort to develop solutions and practices, the poster campaign visualises this collective dynamics as two clasped hands symbolically forming an interactive chain.

LA MARMOTTE
ATELIERS
(SAMEDI)
CAFÉ LE DALAT

8
9
10
05.2015
Théâtre

DO IT TOGETHER
9
8 10
05.2015
Quartier du Vallon
Théâtre 2.21
Journées des alternatives urbaines
Lausanne
alternativesurbaines.ch
LaRevueDurable

DESIGN DAYS 2011

A3 Studio

CL Association Design Days

Organised by interior design magazine Espaces Contemporains, Design Days celebrates contemporary furniture design. In search for a strong element to define the annual event, A3 made the letter D as the identity's focal point with a folded design to give the logo a more technical aspect. The posters were designed as a set of two, reminiscent of 1950's Swiss graphic design. When paired side by side, the bold yellow strokes assemble an "A" as the magazine's mark.

espAces
CONTEMPORAINS
présente
3e édition
Design
Days 2011
Genève
Du 22 au 25
septembre
Des expos, des conférences et un circuit design
avec des showrooms ouverts tout le week-end.
Des invités suisses et internationaux :
Matali Crasset, Alberto Alessi, etc.
Des lieux phares :
Auditorium Arditi, Freestudios, Curiositas,
Haute Ecole d'Art et de Design.
www.designdays.ch
— HEAD
HAUTE ÉCOLE D'ART ET
DE DESIGN GENÈVE
GENEVA UNIVERSITY
OF ART AND DESIGN
ARCHI
TONIC
FONDATION IKEA (SUISSE)

DESIGN DAYS 2014

A3 Studio

CL Association Design Days

Referencing last century's Modernist graphic style, the visual identity of Design Days's 2014 edition manifests a resolutely minimalist spirit. Plain colours, a serif Swiss typeface, gradient and geometric shapes keep the language precise, drawing audience's attention back to the very essence of design. The Ds taken from the event's name intertwine to signify the absence of boundaries within design.

- 183 -

HVALSTRANDFESTIVALEN
Commando Group

CL Håland, Eidsvåg & Strøm

Loud and compelling, Hvalstrandfestivalen's identity draws on maritime signal flags and codes to tie the event with its picturesque seaside venue. The music festival welcomes an audience of all ages, inspiring an adorable tricolour design with a varied geometric pattern boosting a party vibe across its tickets, mementos and decoration. The design is set to evolve year by year. A playful typeface completes the concept on a pleasant note.

- 185 -

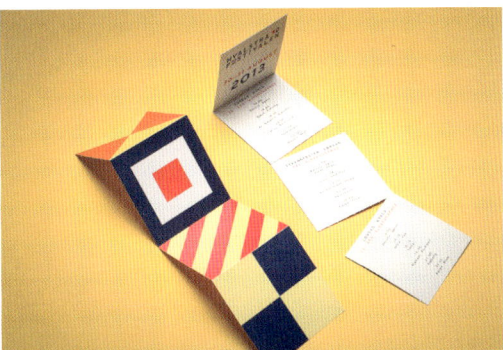

ART.FAB.LAB

innoise

CL K11 Hong Kong

ART.FAB.LAB is makers' workshop, exhibition and seminar space rolled into one. Focusing on digital fabrication and its role in art and design, the event offered a platform where artists and the public can interact and get to know the new model of local production with die-cutting and 3D printing techniques. With a recurring motif, the visual system aims to extend a warm welcome and lure passers-by to the event.

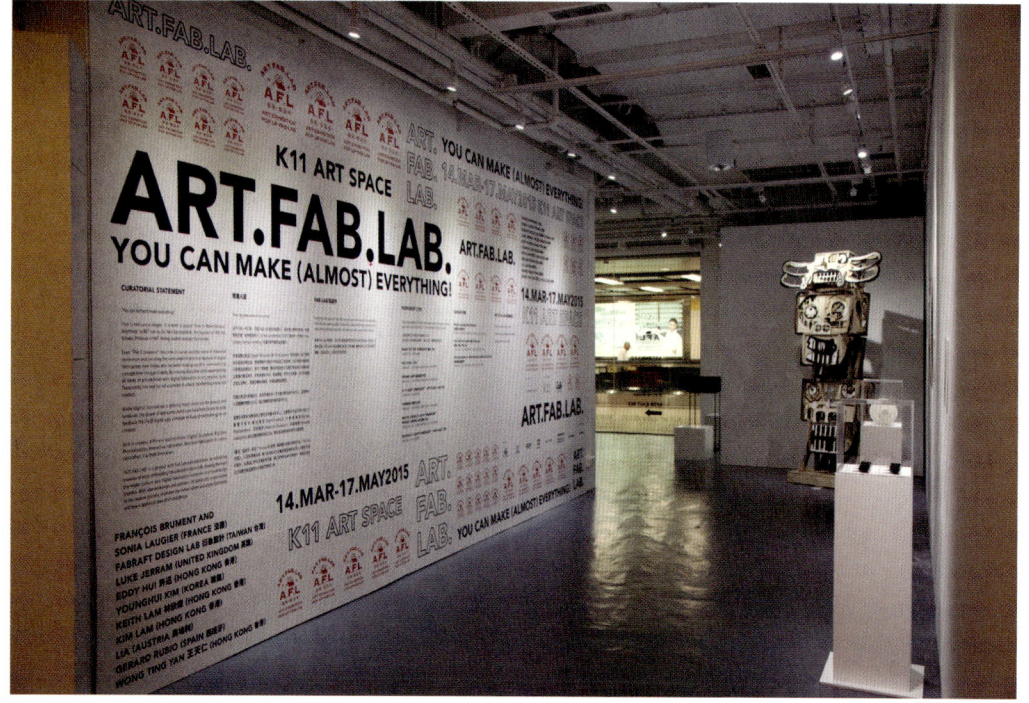

ART.FAB.LAB.

YOU CAN MAKE (ALMOST) EVERYTHING!

K11 ART SPACE
14.MAR-17.MAY 2015
THOUGH B2 D-MOP ZONE / MTR EXIT N3
經 B2 D-MOP ZONE 入 / 港鐵 N3 出口

FRANÇOIS BRUMENT AND
SONIA LAUGIER (FRANCE 法國)
FABRAFT DESIGN LAB 衍象設計 (TAIWAN 台灣)
LUKE JERRAM (UNITED KINGDOM 英國)
EDDY HUI 許迅 (HONG KONG 香港)
YOUNGHUI KIM (KOREA 韓國)
KEITH LAM 林欣傑 (HONG KONG 香港)
KIM LAM (HONG KONG 香港)
LIA (AUSTRIA 奧地利)
GERARD RUBIO (SPAIN 西班牙)
WONG TING YAN 王天仁 (HONG KONG 香港)

K11 ART MALL
18 HANOI ROAD
TSIM SHA TSUI
KOWLOON
HONG KONG
K11 ART SPACE
K11 購物藝術館
香港九龍尖沙咀河內道18號

A.F.L －藝術・製造所－
ART EXHIBITION POP UP FAB LAB

DESIGNED BY INNOISE

PEAR ECO
Futura

CL A. Roland Row

Pear Eco is an Australian organic food label in Taiwan. An earthy tone, kraft paper and a no-frills design call attention to its product's sheer quality rooted in its all-natural and handmade nature. Together with the metallic finishing and a leaf-shaped tag, the visual identity injects credibility into Pear Eco's brand image that speaks to the increasingly health-conscious consumer market.

Pear Eco

Pear Eco
Australian Raw Honey
2X A DAY = HEALTHY
PEAR-ECO.COM

Pear Eco
Ashley Smith
32 JOHNSTON STREET,
MELBOURNE, AUSTRALIA
PEAR-ECO.COM

Pear Eco
Australian Almonds
Pear Eco
Australian Almonds

DÉ-CONNECTONS

Claire Susie Jane

CR Le Corbusier - School of Architecture, Construction and Design

Dé-connectons aimed to raise public awareness of the consequences of smartphone addiction. Taking on a more casual tone, Claire Susie Jane's idea was to prompt self-reflection through humour and games. Card game, stamp and protocol book were provided to help players invent their own solutions to the highlighted problems or simply discuss it in groups.

16 èmes
Journées Mondiales
Sans Téléphone Portable
& Smartphone
À / AU / AUX LA LIBRAIRIE KLÉBER
ATELIERS
CONFÉRENCES
DÉBATS
ON DÉCR-OCHE!
6 10H-12H / 15H-17H
7
8 17H-19H30
FEVRIER 2016
retrouvez toutes les informations sur le site de l'événement
// WWW.LESJOURNEESMONDIALES.COM/
& SUR// WWW. LIBRAIRIE-KLEBER.COM /

16 èmes
Journées Mondiales
Sans Téléphone Portable
& Smartphone
À / AU / AUX LA MÉDIATHÈQUE MALRAUX
ATELIERS
CONFÉRENCES
DÉBATS
ON DÉCR-OCHE!
6 DE 13H30 À 17H30
7
8 DÈS 16H
FEVRIER 2016
retrouvez toutes les informations sur le site de l'événement
// WWW.LESJOURNEESMONDIALES.COM/
& SUR// WWW. MEDIATHEQUES-CUS.FR /

16 èmes
Journées Mondiales
Sans Téléphone Portable
& Smartphone
À / AU / AUX SÉRIES-GRAPHIQUES
ATELIERS
CONFÉRENCES
(DÉBATS)
ON DÉCR-OCHE!
6 DE 14H30 À 17H
7 DE 16H30 À 18H30
8
FEVRIER 2016
retrouvez toutes les informations sur le site de l'événement
// WWW.LESJOURNEESMONDIALES.COM/
& SUR// WWW. SERIES-GRAPHIQUES.COM /

16 èmes
Journées Mondiales
Sans Téléphone Portable
& Smartphone
À / AU / AUX SHADOK
ATELIERS
CONFÉRENCES
DÉBATS
ON DÉCR-OCHE!
6 À PARTIR DE 10H - JUSQU'À 15H
7 DE 10H À MIDI
8 DE 17H À 18H30
FEVRIER 2016
retrouvez toutes les informations sur le site de l'événement
// WWW.LESJOURNEESMONDIALES.COM/
& SUR// WWW. SHADOK.STRASBOURG.EU /

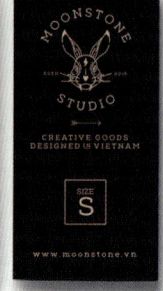

MOONSTONE
CREATIVE STUDIO

HYPE Studio

CL MoonStone Creative Studio

MoonStone Creative Studio is an independent apparel and creative goods brand from Hanoi, Vietnam. The label's logo revives the design of old-time trademarks and features a devilish rabbit as mascot ringed in MoonStone's name and establishment year. In keeping with its cool boy look, the brand's stationery and packaging adopt a solemn duo tone palette set off by gold-foiled details.

MOONSTONE
ESTD 2015
STUDIO

MOONSTONE
ESTD 2015
STUDIO
101 Hare Valley Street
Three Greens Monument District
0164 671 9095
movethestone@gmail.com
www.moonstone.com.vn

SMALL
180,000
VND
www.moonstone.com.vn
MOONSTONE
STUDIO

MUSETTE BAKERY

Judit Besze

Branding for Musette Bakery emphasises on the sheer quality of their tasty bread and pastries. The visual packaging traces the reason back to its traditional practices, with craft paper suggestive of the rustic charm of their freshly-baked bread and a chequer design evocative of a conventional home kitchen where the products are prepared. An upright type and a neutral palette run through the design with a hint of authenticity.

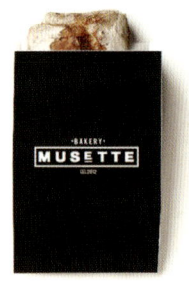

·BAKERY·
MUSETTE
LOVE,
LIFE,
FOOD,
BAKERY,
SUNSHINE,
ENJOY IT!
THOMAS JONES
WWW.MUSETTE.COM

·BAKERY·
MUSETTE
EST. 2012

SEAFARERS

Inhouse Design

CL Northwest Holdings

A brand overhaul has been conceived for Seafarers Building in Auckland's Britomart precinct following a major renovation in 2014. Before being modernised as an entertainment and business hub, the 1970s building was home to global maritime welfare charity, The Mission to Seafarers, which gives it its name. The new identity also honours its past, reflecting a close tie with the nautical culture running from its emblem to its environmental graphics with a vintage flair.

PIVOVARNA 1713

Milos Milovanovic

CL 1713 Pivovarna d.o.o - Tadej Feregotto

Slovenian micro-brewery Pivovarna 1713 is named after the 1713 Tolmin peasant revolt that took place near the brewery's location at the Soča Valley. Asked to build a brand to reference the historical uprising that speaks to drinkers aged around 18-25, Milos Milovanovic created The Bloody Executioner, Cheating Tax Collector, Rebellious Peasant and Greedy Emperor to represent each beer type. Like the beer, everyone has an outstanding character, with visual cues tracing back to the 18th century world.

- 198 -

HOTEL TROFANA ALPIN

Bureau Rabensteiner

CL Nadine Von der Thannen

Trofana Alpin is a traditional family-run hotel in Ischgl, a popular ski destination in Austria. Bureau Rabensteiner was commissioned to modernise the hotel's brand and has aimed for a look and feel that focuses on their exemplary ability to promote tradition with comfort, convenience and spare elegance. Where a balance was achieved by mixing vintage images, woodcut-style illustrations and a clean type, the presence of wood suggests the hotel's proximity to the woods.

LE PAIN BOULE

artless Inc.

CL YAMATO co. Ltd.

Branding and the package design for Japanese artisanal bakery Le pain Boule was crafted to embrace the refined sensibility of the artisans. The delicate flavour of the baked goods made from carefully selected ingredients is graphically translated into a tidy script and an upright functional type "Brandon" which, together with kraft paper, adds warmth and tactility to the brand. Royal blue complements the down-to-earth character with understated sophistication.

le pain Boule
SINCE 2013
FRUIT JAM
いちご

le pain Boule
SINCE 2013
FRUIT JAM

le pain Boule
NACHA COFFEE
CLASSIC

le pain Boule
SINCE 2013
FRUIT JAM

le pain Boule
SINCE 2013
FRUIT JAM

RED KAP

Perky Brothers, LLC, redpepper

CL Red Kap

Workwear manufacturer Red Kap has asked for a lasting imprint to impress the 300 distributors to coincide with the introduction of their new Crew Shirt. Instead of a standard sample descriptions, stories were told, by 300 hard-working target wearers who tested the shirt and shared their experience at first hand. The legitimacy of these taken steps is encapsulated in handwritings and individual's story on a tag and stamps, turning the item into a powerful marketing tool.

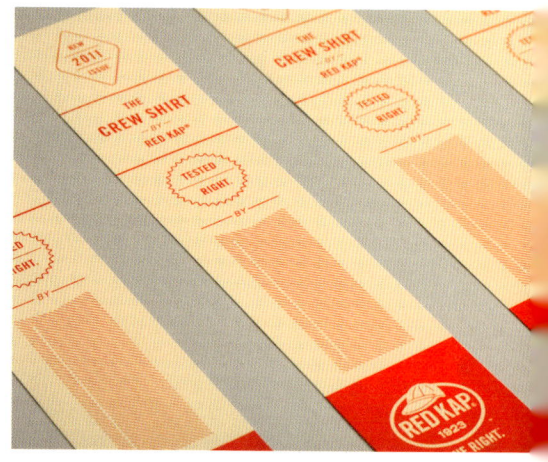

- 203 -

TENDERLOIN MUSEUM

Mucho

CL Tenderloin Museum

The Tenderloin Museum's committed to chronicling the rich history of the San Francisco neighbourhood once peopled by immigrants and iconoclasts, artists and activists, sinners and saints. Visual identity for the museum captures the area's storied past, with mixed type styles borrowed from classic street signs and shop signs evocative of "girls, gambling and graft". A woodblock font further illustrates the gritty nature of Tenderloin, resulting in an eclectic identity that only the museum could own.

- 205 -

ZACH & RACHEL

Yondr Studio

CL Zachary & Rachel Yoder

Having designed wedding invitations for three of his sisters, Nathan Yoder kept this "family tradition" up and running by doing the same for his little brother. Bringing his specialty of illustration and lettering into play, he originated an invite in a retro design with pen and ink which is later realised in offset lithograph. Hand drawn portraits of the bride and groom-to-be and its surrounding variegated lettering compose a layout with visual richness that exudes festivity.

BEE & BLOOM

Yondr Studio

CL Bee & Bloom

Beekeeping and healthy eating blog Bee & Bloom manifests that simplicity originates quality of life. To this end, the blog's visual identity was kept to a minimal, dominated by three stripes and a transfigured ampersand sign to reference a bee and convey the idea of the focus on natural lifestyle. Monochrome print and the use of unbleached paper cohere with the idea in a neat and simple way.

HORRORIS CAVSA

DELINCUENTE MXXXCAL

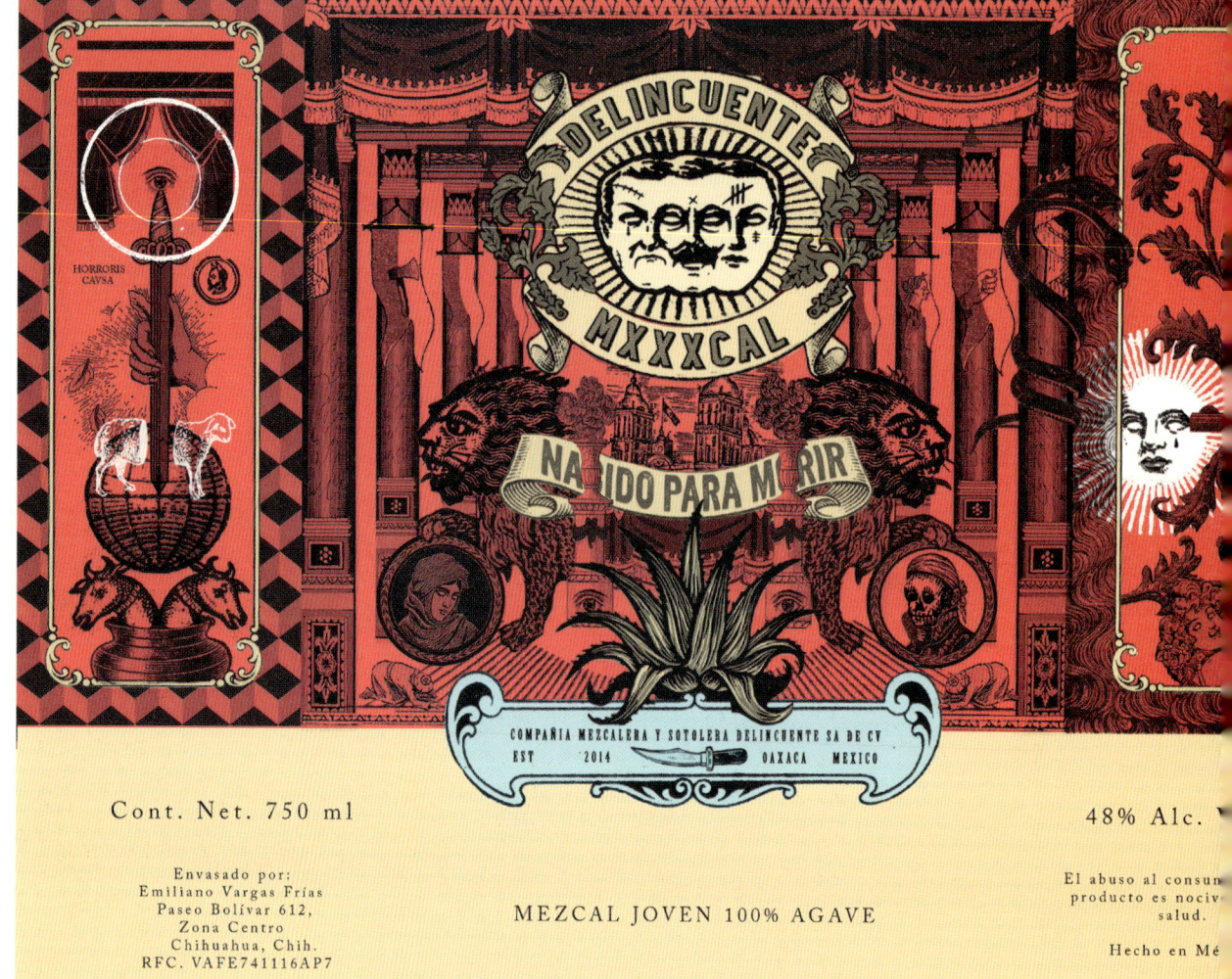

NACIDO PARA MORIR

COMPAÑIA MEZCALERA Y SOTOLERA DELINCUENTE SA DE CV
EST 2014 OAXACA MEXICO

Cont. Net. 750 ml

Envasado por:
Emiliano Vargas Frías
Paseo Bolívar 612,
Zona Centro
Chihuahua, Chih.
RFC. VAFE741116AP7

MEZCAL JOVEN 100% AGAVE

48% Alc.

El abuso al consum
producto es nociv
salud.

Hecho en Mé

Extraído en O

DELINCUENTE
Estudio Yeyé

Delincuente produces mezcal, a native liquor from Mexico. Referencing the beverage's origin and the nation's notable high crime rate, the packaging solution honours drug trades and poverty with an economic wrapper where quirky hybrids and semi-transparent overlays create a hallucinating effect of drugs on a user. A logo featuring morphing faces and tally marks vaguely suggestive of crime figures reinforces the concept.

GUIMARÃES JAZZ 2011
POSTERS

Non-Verbal Club

IL Aleksandra Niepsuj
CL Centro Cultural Vila Flor

Strikingly infectious, Guimarães Jazz 2011's poster design celebrated both the return of the Portuguese music festival and its 20th birthday at once. Futurism and Dada influences were key to what Non-Verbal Club had in mind, who then collaborated with illustrator Aleksandra Niepsuj, who helped bring a certain naivety to the contrasting look the designers wanted to express. The result was three enthusiastic designs, each engaging in a visually rhythmic way.

Quinta 10
The Roy Haynes Fountain
of Youth Band
Sexta 11
The Swallow Quintet
Sábado 12
Cedar Walton Trio
CENTRO CULTURAL VILA FLOR
GUIMARÃES
GUIMARÃES 2012
CAPITAL EUROPEIA DA CULTURA
WWW.CCVF.PT
M/12

Quinta 10
The Roy Haynes Fountain
of Youth Band
Sexta 11
The Swallow Quintet
Sábado 12
Cedar Walton Trio
Domingo 13
Projecto Toap/Guimarães Jazz 2011
Akiko Pavolka, Bernardo Moreira, Jochen
Rueckert, Nate Radley, Óscar Graça
20 anos
GUIMARÃES
JAZZ
NOV
08
19
Quarta 16
Ralph Alessi and This
Against That with
Tony Malaby, Andy Milne,
Drew Gress and Mark Ferber
Quinta 17
McCoy Tyner Trio
With Special Guests Jose James & Chris Potter
Sexta 18
Henry Threadgill & Zooid
Sábado 19
William Parker "Essence of Ellington"
Sábado 19
Ralph Alessi dirige Big Band da ESMAE
CENTRO CULTURAL VILA FLOR
GUIMARÃES
GUIMARÃES 2012
CAPITAL EUROPEIA DA CULTURA
WWW.CCVF.PT
M/12

FORMOSA MEDICINE SHOW
Onion Design Associates

CL The Muddy Basin Ramblers

The Muddy Basin Ramblers is a Taiwanese jug band specialising in old time jazz, blues and ragtime. With their album's concept rooted in 1920s local medicine shows, Onion Design put forward a solution that stays true to the illustrated bilingual ads popular at the time. Titled "Formosa Medicine Show", the album is wrapped in a 45-RPM sleeve, completed with a vintage classified-ad looking design that unfolds the song's lyrics.

- 213 -

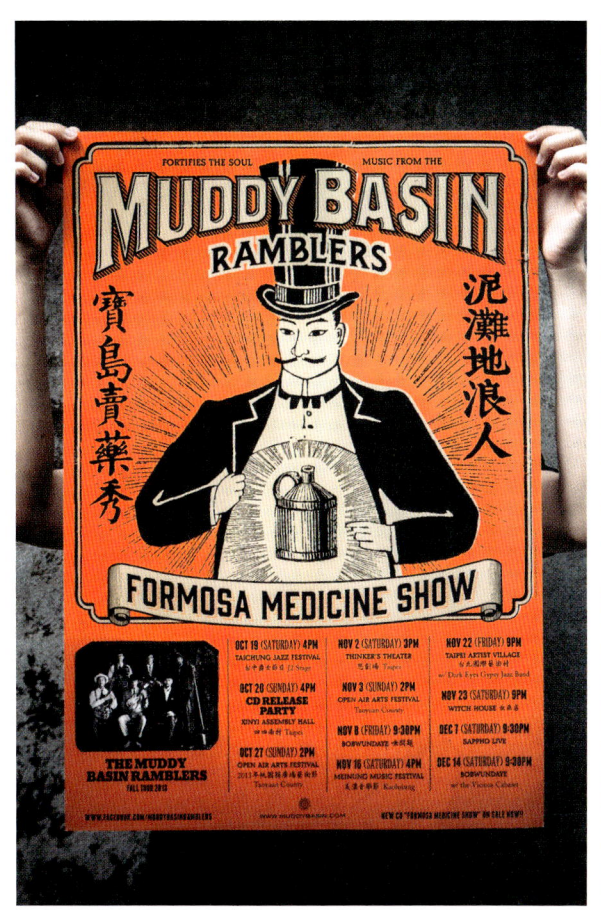

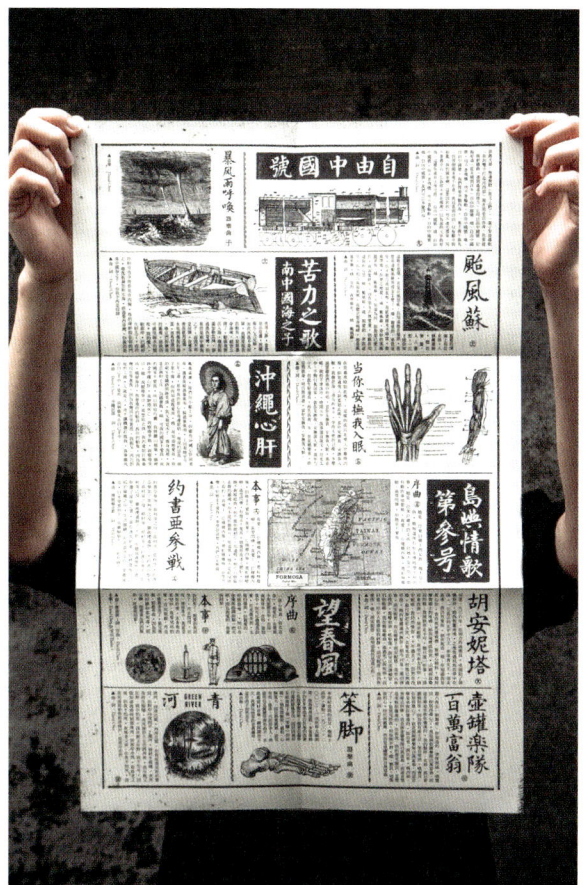

THE ADVERTISEMENT SAYS

Wang Zhi-Hong Studio

CL Rye Field Publications

Titled "The Advertisement Says", the book examines modern Taiwanese life through advertisements arose during Japanese colonial rule. In an attempt to evoke how old brands, trendy products and strategic marketing campaigns overpower consumers, Wang put together a tabloid-size jacket where a chaotic mass of archived print graphics almost buries the book's title. Each piece picked makes for an exquisite showcase of vintage illustrations, text arrangement and logos that Wang holds dear.

東京松竹少女歌劇
丸山和歌子
と來演
壹圓均一
味の素
使ふとテモ
まくて経済
月賦販賣
バスケット靴
クレープ底
白衣
運動靴
亀甲萬醤油
バニシングの
眞の意味！
特選靴
運のよい人は僅か
一圓の御買物で
花の内地の觀光が
出來ます
カルピス
プラトン
シヤープー鉛筆
血色を良くし
体重を増加す
クレープ底
運動靴
虎標
信州伊那の谷特産
養命酒
三百年の
廣告表示：
COW'S HEAD BRAND
CONDENSED MILK
G. KONISHI
OSAKA & KOBE
臺灣日日新報
The Advertisement Says:
Old Brands, Chic Goods, Marketing Strategies.
A Look at the Modern Life of Taiwan Through
Advertisements During Japanese Colonial Period
陳柔縉
著
麥田出版
ISBN 978-986-344-242-4 NT$990 HK$330 RV1076
森永
ミルクキャラメル
全家庭に
花王のマーク
ハモニカ
大粒
小粒仁丹
脱毛剤
エブ
若禿拔け毛
防止に
ヨウモトニック
キャラメル
健胃固腸丸
SUN-RISE
MURAI'S
SUN-RISE
CIGARETTES
MURAI BROS & CO.
KYOTO, JAPAN.
HERO
HERO
CIGARETTES
MANUFACTURED BY
MURAI BROS & CO.
KYOTO, JAPAN.
MURAI'S HERO

SPARKLE STUDIO

Violaine & Jérémy

PH Olivia Fremineau
CL Sparkle

Sparkle Studio is a creative partnership between music producers David Dahan and Joseph Guigui. Driven to contrive contemporary soundscapes with rare vintage equipment, the Parisian music production studio conceived a basic diamond-shaped logo with a prominent vintage quality to match the name "Sparkle" that can be used alone or paired with the owners in their very nice suits. The intricate illustrations add a fashionable touch.

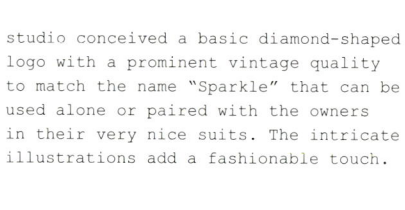

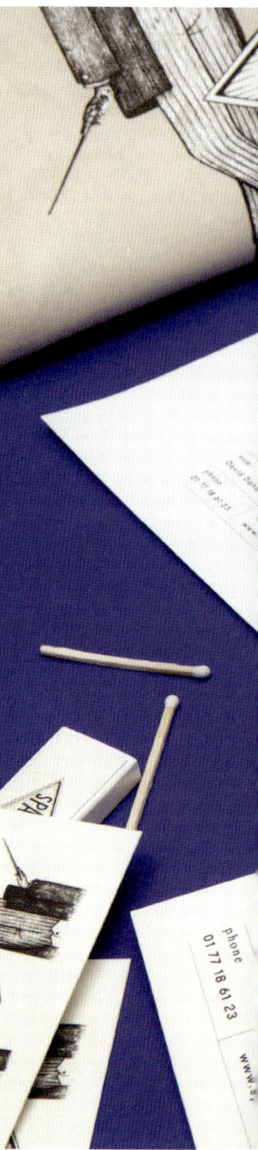

David Dahan
email
david@sparklestudio.fr
phone
01 77 18 61 23
web
www.sparklestudio.fr

RECORDS
SPARKLE
STUDIO
David Dahan
email
david@sparklestudio.fr
phone
01 77 18 61 23
web
www.sparklestudio.fr
David Dahan

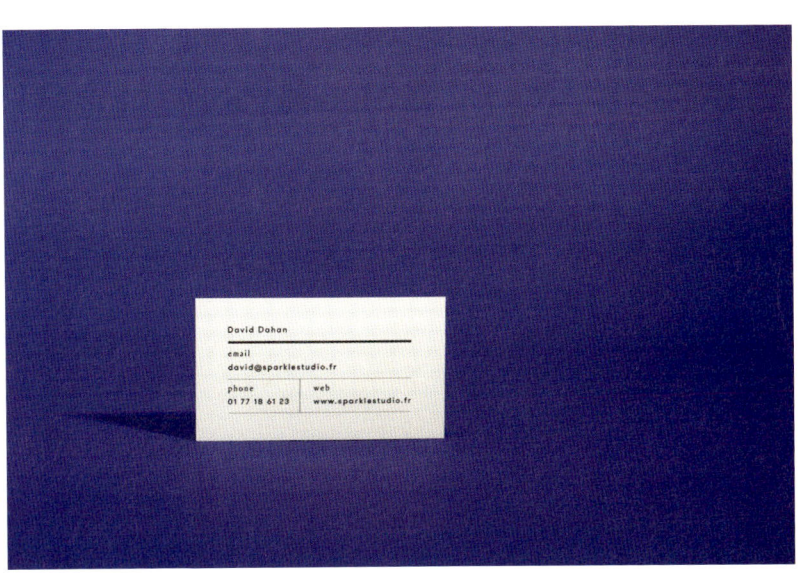

THE SECRET DONUT SOCIETY

Ceci Peralta, José Velázquez

A hidden gem in San Pedro Garza Garcia, The Secret Donut Society sells donuts characterised by bold flavours ensconced in a basement. The store is named by designers Ceci Peralta and José Velázquez, who also developed its brand identity that sustains the business' eccentric charisma. Referencing the Masons and Illuminati, the duo created a visual identity system that would mesmerise donut buffs.

- 219 -

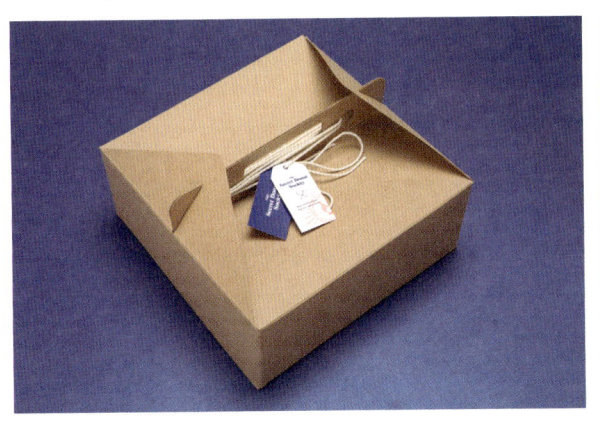

THE CLIFFORD PIER
Foreign Policy Design Group

CL The Clifford Pier

Named from the bustling port at Marina Bay in the 1930s, The Clifford Pier is a Singapore-based restaurant serving contemporary Southeast Asian cuisine. The port's legacy was a major inspiration for the restaurant's visual identity, with a ginger flower motif to honour the country's botany that once fascinated General William Farquhar during his stay on the island. Classic postage stamps, sea-trip elements, a marine-inspired palette and food illustrations resembling Farquhar's remarkable collection of natural history drawings round up the idea as an homage to the historic waterfront landmark.

POSTCARD
THE CLIFFORD PIER
1¢
POSTAGE
THE CLIFFORD PIER SINGAPORE 1933
THE CLIFFORD PIER SINGAPORE 1933
+65 6597 5266
+65 6597 5218
CLIFFORDPIER@FULLERTONBAYHOTEL.COM
THE FULLERTON BAY HOTEL
80 COLLYER QUAY
REPUBLIC OF SINGAPORE
049326
THIS TICKET
ENTITLES THE
BEARER TO ENTER
ON 3RD JUNE 2014
THANK YOU FOR CELEBRATING
THE PIER'S 81ST
ANNIVERSARY WITH US
No. 135
ADMIT ONE
THE CLIFFORD PIER SINGAPORE

REPUBLIC OF SINGAPORE
049326
THE CLIFFORD PIER SINGAPORE 1933

ADMIT ONE
THIS TICKET
ENTITLES THE
BEARER TO ENTER
ON 3RD JUNE 2014
THE CLIFFORD PIER
ADMIT ONE

- 222 -

- 223 -

HAYMARKET

Foreign Policy Design Group

CL Hong Kong Jockey Club

Nestled in a British colonial establishment, HayMarket is a meeting point of horse-racing spectators at Hong Kong's Shatin Racecourse. The restaurant's visual identity system is an eclectic mix of vintage British typography, Victorian illustrations commonly found in old advertisements and vibrant graphics that drew on the jockey culture. The logo is a playful update on classic letterforms and functions as a blank canvas, allowing for quirky permutations when combined with different illustrations.

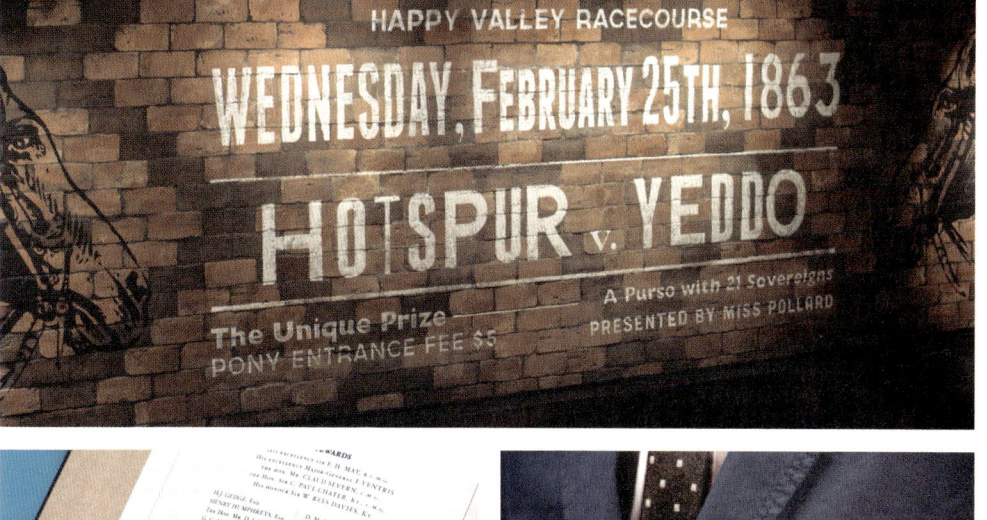

THE LADIES' PURSE
HAPPY VALLEY RACECOURSE

WEDNESDAY, FEBRUARY 25TH, 1863

HOTSPUR v. YEDDO

The Unique Prize — PONY ENTRANCE FEE $5

A Purse with 21 Sovereigns
PRESENTED BY MISS POLLARD

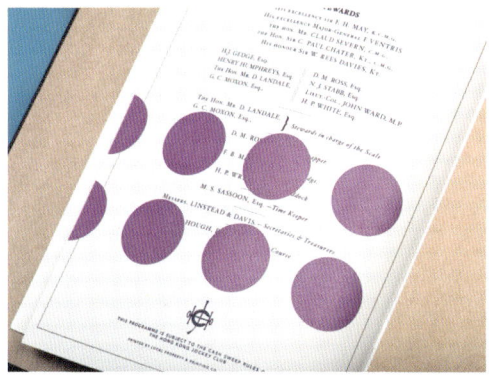

- 225 -

EL CAMINO FOODTRUCK

Savvy Studio

PH Alejandro Cartagena
CL Desarrollos Gómez

El Camino Foodtruck answers to Monterrey's gastronomic needs. Combining Spanish and English, its name subtly communicates its transcultural flavours that extends to its typographic approach, expressing the truck's rough and Texan personality appealingly with reference to Americana and biker tattoo designs. The variety of writing style drawn up by hand highlights El Camino's artisanal cooking and its wide-ranging menu featuring burgers and vegetarian food.

- 227 -

- 228 -

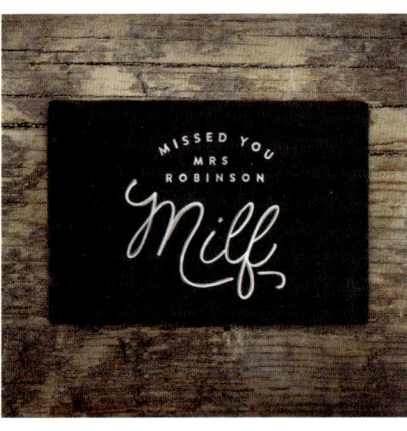

ONE OF A KIND
Don't Try Studio

A visual exploration of slang terms for women, One of a Kind graphically interprets various common expressions in illustrations, pictures and mixed typography. Stripping any conceivable kind of offensive remarks, these images turn the focus back to the neutral qualities these words imply. Models dressed and posed as iconic pin-up girls and celebrities from the fifties suggest the tradition of using these slangs in daily language.

RIVADAVIA
MONOTYPO Studio

CL Cecilia de Quiroz

Put together as a fanciful platter of fresh and delicious food, branding for Italian-Argentinian restaurant RIVADAVIA draws inspirations from a diverse source. The logo with a cow suckling two men was a variant of Capitoline Wolf from Roman mythology, Romulus and Remus, but the system also features a fusion of food and related imagery that concoct a collective brand image united by detailed drawings.

- 231 -

PIG'S PEARLS

MONOTYPO Studio

CL PIG´S PEARLS

Influences of Victorian age graphic style and 19th century English engravings prevail the visual identity of PIG's PEARLS, a gourmet burger restaurant in Guadalajara, Mexico. Fine drawings of a historic kitchen and a thoughtful brand approach immediately set the restaurant apart from other local fast food joints. The illustrations also hint at the use of fresh and premium ingredients that give the food its distinguishing flavours.

BIÈRES DU CHÂTEAU

A3 Studio

PH Michel Meier
CL Brasserie Artisanale du château Lausanne

Lausanne-based brewery Bières du château's beer are brewed in the most traditional way. For this reason A3 Studio has developed a graphic style which is both contemporary and traditional. The labels reference the sea world and are decorated with ropes. Where hand drawn illustrations emphasise the handmade production process inspired by old engravings and sailor tattoos, craft paper stresses the authenticity of the beer.

THE SUPERNATURAL
Inhouse Design

CL And Co. Wines

Playing on the wine's name, The Supernatural's bottle label was imagined as a cabinet of curiosities featuring taxidermy, apparatuses and otherworldly objects drawn from natural history. The idea continues on, with the beer's aroma references and the brewer's belief dancing across the label. A monochrome and metallic gold palette gives the beverage a tint of extra flavour.

- 235 -

THE SICILIAN
Bravo

CL The Sicilian

The Sicilian serves revived Italian cuisine in New South Wales, Australia. Accompanying recipes from the 1940s is a brand system that references American gangster movie setting of the same era when food, money and family took priority. The theme runs seamlessly from dollar note-like vouchers to its tabloid-inspired breakfast menu, with TV fictional character Don Corleone making the headline. The typographic logo is crafted from the engraved inscriptions of firearms and the monogram of the shield, from an open gun chamber.

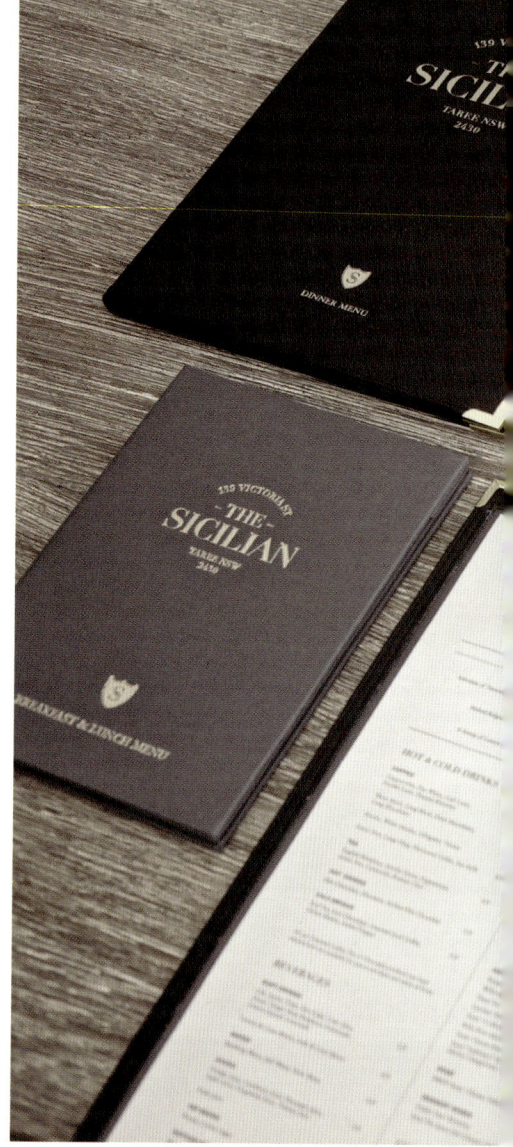

THE SICILIAN
RESTAURANT & BAR
Our Breakfast Menu
THE SICILIAN
THE DAMAGE

THE SICILIAN
RESTAURANT
& BAR
KB 46279860 I

BAR GINGER
Power-nap Over

CL Bar Ginger

A logo and a customised logotype express medieval influences that subtly conforms with Bar Ginger's prohibition-style interior. Depicting a ladder leaning against a letter G, the sign invites the whisky bar's clientele to enter another side of the world for a pure journey of taste. A metallic and navy blue palette sets the mood for an unforgettable night out.

- 239 -

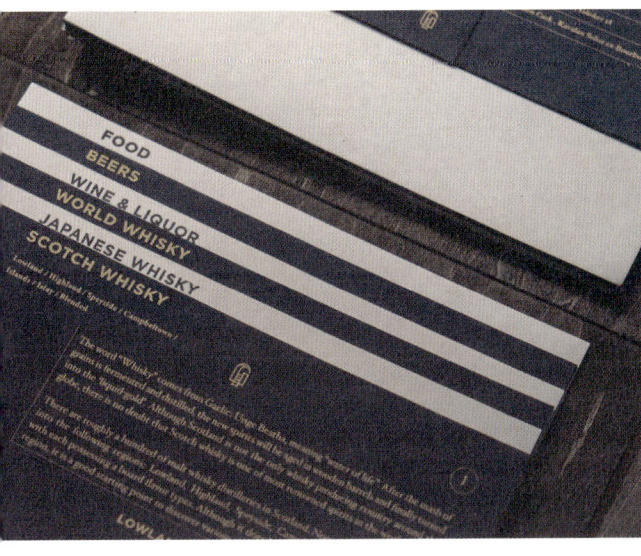

- 240 -

LUCHA LOCO
Bravo

CL Lucha Loco

With a moniker borrowed from the famous Mexican wrestler, Lucha Loco is a taqueria and bar that serves authentic Mexican street food in Singapore. Aiming for a rustic appearance as if the young bar has existed for decades, the restaurant's brand applications give way to a burst of Lucha Libra cultural cues, complimented by simple designed elements, such as a logo depicting a luchador performing an "Asai Moonsault". The business cards resembling vintage trading cards of wrestling celebs add a humorous touch.

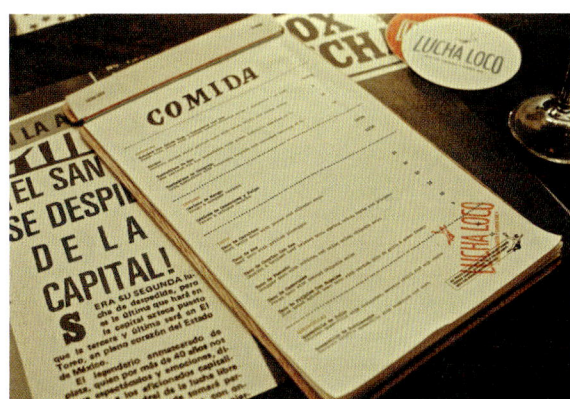

HOTEL CYCLE
UMA/design farm

IN SUPPOSE DESIGN OFFICE
PH Yoshiro Masuda
CL Discoverlink Setouchi Inc.

HOTEL CYCLE is part of Onomichi U2, a resort complex dedicated to cycling enthusiasts. The hotel's identity is characterised by a logotype and typesetting that run afloat on the walls, referencing the moment when guests were cycling leisurely around the many slopes in the city of Onomichi city, Hiroshima, Japan. Also an homage to the coastal city's shipbuilding and metalworking heritage, brass plays as an integral element in giving the identity a classic yet industrial look.

- 243 -

THE ASSEMBLY
Bravo

CL Benjamin Barker

The Assembly is a multi-label men's fashion store that also houses a café named The Assembly Ground. Targeting fun-loving and spontaneous gentlemen with an eye to quality, the shop's brand identity is a classic, versatile and playful one that contributes a nostalgic ambience in the retail space. Its logo, resembling the letter 'A' constructed with three sticks, reinforces the retail concept of combining the shop and café as a place of convocation.

- 245 -

SOPRA

Bravo

CL Sopra Cucina & Bar

Sopra Cucina & Bar is an Italian restaurant located at a corner of a busy shopping district in Jakarta. To put neighbouring night entertainment establishments in the shade, Bravo found inspiration in the razzle-dazzle of postwar Italian cinema and forged a glamorous identity for the restaurant. Realised as an illuminated grand signage and graphic logo, Sopra is an ode to the glamorous days when Hollywood, Federico Fellini films and Sophia Loren first captured their imaginations.

- 247 -

A3 Studio / Absoloot / Alana Louise / Anna Kövecses / artless Inc. / atelier bingo. / Bravo / Brian Steely / Bunker3022 / Bureau Rabensteiner / Ceci Peralta, José Velázquez / Claire Susie Jane / Colin Miller / Commando Group / David Cran / Diana Orozco / dn&co. / Dock 57 / Don't Try Studio / Duane Dalton / Estudi Àlex Ramon Mas / Estudio Yeyé / Facultative Works / Foreign Policy Design Group / Fundamental-Studio / Futura / Geyser / Hey / HYPE Studio / Inhouse Design / innoise / Jared Bell / Joe Haddad / Judit Besze / Lo Siento / Mads Berg Illustration / Milos Milovanovic / MONOTYPO Studio / Motoi Shito / Mucho / Non-Verbal Club / 0.00 Risograph Printing & Design ROOM / Oddds / Onion Design Associates / Opus Nigrum / Perky Brothers, LLC / Pol Pintó Fabregat / Power-nap Over / Ryan Chapman / Savvy Studio / Say What Studio / Studio Daad, Studio Turbo / studiowmw / Sunday Lounge / Table Six / The Good Folks Co. / Tobias Saul / Tom Grunwald / Tseng Kuo-chan / UMA/design farm / vacaliebres / Violaine & Jérémy / Wang Zhi-Hong Studio / Wing's Art and Design Studio / Yondr Studio / Zdunkiewicz Studio / ZEALPLUS

A3 STUDIO

Consists of graphic designer Yvo Hählen and visual communication designer Priscilla Balmer, A3 produces illustration, graphic design and typography with special attention to its prints quality, while also develops artistic production. Founded in 2011 in Lausanne, Switzerland, A3 is regularly rewarded locally and abroad.

PAGE 140-141, 176-183, 233

ABSOLOOT

A creative studio providing premium print solutions, print consultation and management. Absoloot's passion is quality. They pay close attention to the details of every element of the print process, be it finding the best possible paper, ink or design. They work closely with designers, clients and businesses, combining traditional and innovative solutions to create timeless value and outstanding quality.

PAGE 148-149

ARTLESS INC.

Establised in 2000 by Shun Kawakami, the interdisciplinary design and consulting firm works across all media including brand design, visual and corporate identity, advertising, packaging, product, video and motion graphics. The studio has won international awards including Cannes Gold Lions, NY ADC, D&AD and The London International Award.

PAGE 200-201

ATELIER BINGO.

The studio of Maxime Prou and Adèle Favreau who are both illustrators, surface pattern and graphic designers from France. atelier bingo. loves to experiment with screenprinting and other graphic techniques to create colourful and abstract works.

PAGE 104

BELL, JARED

Bell is a Brooklyn-based musician and designer.

PAGE 122-123

BESZE, JUDIT

Currently living in Budapest, Hungary, Besze started three years ago as a freelance graphic designer. An autodidactic of graphic design, Besze's favourite creative field is food packaging design, besides working on branding projects for cafés, bakeries and restaurants.

PAGE 194-195

BRAVO

Bravo is a creatively-led design studio based in Singapore. Specialising in identity, brand development, printed communications and art direction, the independent workshop works with a variety of individuals and organisations to deliver thoughtful and engaging designs.

PAGE 156-159, 236-237, 240-241, 244-247

BUNKER3022

A branding and design studio based in Buenos Aires, Argentina with a focus on lifestyle and retail industry. Working with clients locally and internationally, Bunker3022 provides complete brand development from communication strategies, naming and consulting, photoshooting to brand promotion. They also take up full identity projects and work on the digital field on content generation and community management for social media.

PAGE 136-137

BUREAU RABENSTEINER

Bureau Rabensteiner is an Austrian design studio specialises in creative direction and graphic design. Since day one, Rabensteiner has always been about quality and detail.

PAGE 198-199

CHAPMAN, RYAN

Chapman is a British illustrator who focuses on the simple use of soft shapes and minimal colours. Chapman has collaborated on a range of projects with clients including Google, The New York Times, Microsoft, eBay and many others.

PAGE 100-101

CLAIRE SUSIE JANE

The studio of Claire Susie Jane, a young graphic designer from Strasbourg, France. Recently gratuated in Global Design and specialises in web design and branding, she has developed a real passion for editorial design. She adopts a global approach on design, allowing her to achieve a wide variety of projects.

PAGE 190-191

COMMANDO GROUP

Commando Group AS specialises in graphic design and illustration. They aim at merging their skills and knowledge into solutions that aid products and companies fighting to be visible and reach the target audience. Commando Group AS strongly believes that all design is strategic.

PAGE 184-185

CRAN, DAVID

Currently based between Vancouver and Seattle, Cran is a designer and illustrator with more than 30 years of experience and a passion for vintage-influenced typography, iconography and branding.

PAGE 026-029

DALTON, DUANE

Studied at The Institute of Art, Design and Technology (IADT), Dalton is a graphic designer and artist from Dublin, Ireland. He is passionate about minimal and reductive design qualities that communicate a clear and precise message. This attribute is common throughout the majority of his work. Currently living and working in London, Dalton is now a designer at SEA Design.

PAGE 098-099

DN&CO.

dn&co. builds brands from the ground up covering print, digital, film and exhibition design. Strong strategic thinking as well as unapologetically modern aesthetics combined with a passion for space and architecture, has ensured the team to create work that is original, appropriate and enduring.

PAGE 128-129

DOCK 57

Dock 57 is two freelance graphic designers from Russia, Sveta Shubina and Manar Shajri, who specialise in creating logotypes, corporate branding and illustrations. The duo has been creating visual identity of the highest quality according to the clients' needs since 2011.

PAGE 076-079

DON'T TRY STUDIO

Multidisciplinary studio based in Paris run by Quentin Monge focusing on branding and illustration.

PAGE 228-229

ESTUDI ÀLEX RAMON MAS

The studio of Àlex Ramon Mas. Based in Barcelona, it specialises and has extensive experience in graphic design, brand and corporate identity, illustration, advertising and web design. Always striving to understand and adapt to each client's specific needs, the studio combines strategy and design with attention to detail to create unique brand experiences in different media.

PAGE 010-021

ESTUDIO YEYÉ

Specialises in graphic design, photography, publicity and illustration, Estudio Yeyé's principal goal is to create relevant, innovative and work of utmost quality that help clients' businesses to grow.

PAGE 208-209

FACULTATIVE WORKS

Facultative Works is founded on the idea of working only with the experimental and fascinating projects during free time for fun. After a while the studio turned into a more significant operation while the main approach on work hasn't change. The studio prefers the holistic approach to design by working in different fields such as illustration, identity, sound, editorial and furniture design.

PAGE 138-139

FOREIGN POLICY DESIGN GROUP

Helmed by creative directors Yah-Leng Yu and Arthur Chin, the group works on projects ranging from creative/art direction and design, branding, brand strategy, digital strategy, strategic research and marketing campaign for luxury fashion and lifestyle brands, FCMG, arts and cultural institutions and think tank consultancies.

PAGE 108-115, 144-147, 220-225

FUNDAMENTAL-STUDIO

Based in Hong Kong, Fundamental believes that substantial communication is the key to creating and providing best designs and solutions to clients.

PAGE 154-155

FUTURA

Futura is a design studio specialising in brand building. Founded by Iván García and Vicky González in 2008, the combination of two different sets of background and working method has given the duo a unique way of approaching projects and finding balance between stiffness and rebellion.

PAGE 188-189

GEYSER

Alias Geyser, Gijs Dries is a Belgium-based visual identity designer and brand builder with a focus on branding, typography and illustration. Fascinated by vintage signage and lettering, Dries contributes his part to the vintage enthusiast community. Known for his minimal and straightforward designs with a retro touch, Dries gets inspiration by looking back in time.

PAGE 040-041

GRUNWALD, TOM

Grunwald was born and raised in New York. He likes art, design, and is going fast on two wheels.

PAGE 084-088

HADDAD, JOE

Haddad is a New York-based multidisciplinary designer. Besides taking a BFA in graphic design at the School of Visual Arts where he intends to graduate in 2017, Haddad is also currently an intern at GrandArmy. Prior to GrandArmy he has worked at Mother New York and Deutsch Inc.

PAGE 130-131

HEY

A multidisciplinary design studio based in Barcelona, Spain. Specialising in brand management and editorial design, packaging and interactive design, Hey shares the profound conviction that good design means combining content, functionality, graphical expression and strategy.

PAGE 106-107

HYPE STUDIO

HYPE Studio is a small design studio based in Hanoi, Vietnam.

PAGE 192-193

INHOUSE DESIGN

Inhouse is an Auckland-based consultancy creating appropriate and effective solutions through simple, clear and well-crafted graphic designs. Founded in 1995, Inhouse is a small practice often collaborating with other creative specialists, artists, architects, product designers and digital experts.

PAGE 196, 234-235

INNOISE

Founded by Jerry Luk in 2010, innoise specialises in branding, art direction, graphic and motion design besides a diverse collection of self-initiated artworks, projects and unique products. Luk believes that a good design not only includes brilliant visuals, but also utilises a product's function and builds a distinctive image for a brand.

PAGE 186-187

KÖVECSES, ANNA

Kövecses is a Hungarian graphic designer living in the small seaside village of Cyprus, where she draws inspirations from. From magazine illustrations to book covers, fashion to fine art, her work is characterised by simple forms and bold colours, merging minimalism with a naive European nostalgia, which often includes alpine landscapes, mountain huts and friendly animals.

PAGE 102-103

LO SIENTO

Founded by Borja Martinez in 2005 and now a team of six, Lo Siento is interested in taking over identity projects as a whole, covering the fields of corporative branding, packaging and editorial design. Their emphasis on materials results in solutions where graphic and industrial design go hand in hand. In 2014, Martinez is nominated to be part of the FAD assembly.

PAGE 126-127

LOUISE, ALANA

Half of The Good Folks Co., Louise is born with two hands and two first names.

PAGE 022

MADS BERG ILLUSTRATION

Graduated from the Danish Design School in 2001, Berg has been working independently as an illustrator while occasionally being a lecturer at design schools and an award jury. Characterised by a style which translates classic poster art into a modern and timeless look, Berg won the Danish Design Prize in 2009 and the "Best Danish Children's Comic" prize in 2010.

PAGE 118-119

MILLER, COLIN

Half of The Good Folks Co., Miller is a keystoner and a huge Weakerthans fan.

PAGE 022-024

MILOVANOVIC, MILOS

Milovanovic is an award-winning graphic designer based in Serbia. His designs tend to lean on the illustrative side with a vintage, retro feel to it. The main focus of his craft is to reflect essence, culture and personality of each client, creating interesting illustrative pieces that include logos, emblems, labels and packagings.

PAGE 034-039, 197

MONOTYPO STUDIO

MONOTYPO is a business service agency specialising in visual communication and graphic design. The main objective is to leave a graphic impression of cleanliness, simplicity, aesthetics and functionality while satisfying clients' needs by in-depth analysis and tailor-made solutions.

PAGE 032-033, 080-083, 230-232

MUCHO

A studio expertised in art direction, strategic and corporate identity, editorial design, packaging, communications, digital design and motion graphics.

PAGE 204-205

NON-VERBAL CLUB

Formerly known as Atelier Martino & Jaña, Non-Verbal is a communication design studio based in Porto, Portugal. Obsessed with books, visual systems and typography, the team is vastly experienced in multidisciplinary design projects and have worked with notable clients such as Nike USA, NBC USA, European Capitals of Culture, The Vila Flor Cultural Centre, Porto City Hall, among many others.

PAGE 105, 116-117, 210-211

O.OO RISOGRAPH PRINTING & DESIGN ROOM

The Taiwan-based studio is founded in 2014 by Pip Lu who graduated from Shih Chien University's Department of Communications Design. With an addiction to Risograph printing, Lu is also an visual artist of installation art and graphic design.

PAGE 132-135, 174-175

ODDDS

Founded in 2013 by designers based in Penang and Singapore respectively, Oddds focuses on graphic design, branding, photography, publication design, and illustration. Their work reflects significantly on behaviours, including how it draws attention and how it influences people. The team believes in aesthetics and futurism.

PAGE 090-091, 162-163

ONION DESIGN ASSOCIATES

A multidisciplinary graphic design studio co-founded by Andrew Wong in Taipei, Taiwan.

PAGE 212-213

OPUS NIGRUM

The work name of Gabriel Oviedo. Currently working at an advertising agency as a senior graphic designer, it is his personal work that has achieved transcendence, with only him judging.

PAGE 052-057

OROZCO, DIANA

Orozco is a graphic designer and digital marketer with more than seven years of experience in logo design. She has worked with clients from the United States, Australia, Switzerland, the UK and Latin America. She is the founder and director of HeyDesign Magazine.

PAGE 064-069

PERALTA, CECI, VELÁZQUEZ, JOSÉ

Peralta and Velázquez attended design school together, became friends and from then on started working as a team. The duo developed most school projects together and realised a nice vibe going on. Later they went separate ways upon graduation but still try working together on some specific projects professionally.

PAGE 218-219

PERKY BROTHERS, LLC

Founded in 1883 and transformed its services in 2009, Perky Brothers now exists to help both startup and established brands to gain clarity, value and distinction through design, visual identities, websites, packaging, print materials and any odd or end necessary for an authentic experience. The studio calls Nashville, Tennessee their home.

PAGE 202-203

PINTÓ FABREGAT, POL

Studied at Eina University and worked with Esiete, PFP disseny grafic, Pintó Fabregat is currently working with Dani Rubio Arauna on corporate identity, communication strategy, editorial design, exhibitions and signage projects.

PAGE 124-125, 170-173

POWER-NAP OVER

Founded in Hong Kong by Vita Mak in 2013, the studio works across a diverse range of projects including art direction, branding, editorial, event, packaging and website design. At the same time the team also develops home products and independent publications. They intend to use products, graphics and text to express opinions about living.

PAGE 238-239

SAUL, TOBIAS

Saul is a lettering artist and graphic designer from Düsseldorf, Germany. Started with graffiti and illustration at an early age, his passion for letters and layouts continued while he studied communication design with a focus on logo, branding and packaging. All of his work begins with pen and paper and digitalised later for finishing touches.

PAGE 060-063

SAVVY STUDIO

A multidisciplinary studio dedicated to developing brand experiences that generate emotions between clients and target audience. Composed of specialists in marketing, communication, graphic design, industrial design, creative copywriting and architecture, Savvy Studio also collaborates with talented artists and designers worldwide.

PAGE 226-227

SAY WHAT STUDIO

Say What Studio is a graphic design studio based in Paris that runs by Benoit Berger and Nathalie Kapagiannidi. Bound by a common passion, the pair founded the studio after graduating from the ECV school in 2011.

PAGE 050-051

SHITO, MOTOI

Shito is an art director and graphic designer based in Tokyo, Japan.

PAGE 120-121

STEELY, BRIAN

Steely is an American designer widely known for his unique line logos. His work reinforces that it is not only the graphics that begin unravelling what a company does, but also the style it was created in. Using simple line-art, he manages to produce a range of diverse and inspiring logo designs for a number of outlets. From food products to bike head badges, his style works for every single one.

PAGE 070-075

STUDIO DAAD, STUDIO TURBO

Studio Daad and Studio Turbo are both typography-based design studios from the Netherlands. The work of Studio Daad mostly represents itself as handcrafted designs, while the work of Studio Turbo is mostly digital created.

PAGE 142-143

STUDIOWMW

A design agency based in Hong Kong with footsteps in the global marketplace founded by Sunny Wong. Specialises in brand building, studiowmw's work ranges from identity to environmental design, from packaging to product design, from website to physical store, from commerce to charity. studiowmw believes mutual trust and relationships are the key to successful brands.

PAGE 150-153

SUNDAY LOUNGE

The studio of Jared Jacob who lives and works in Salida, Colorado, USA.

PAGE 042-049

TABLE SIX

Table Six is an agile graphic design studio from Jakarta, Indonesia. The versatile characteristic as a team of creatives, leads them to interesting clients from different industries. They indulge themselves in doing what they love, and they love to collaborate with passionate people alike who believe in their products or services.

PAGE 164-167

THE GOOD FOLKS CO.

The work name of Colin Miller and Alana Louise who claim themselves five foot small and six foot tall.

PAGE 025

TSENG, KUO-CHAN

The Taiwanese graphic designer was born in 1990 in Tainan, Taiwan. Graduated in visual communication design from National Yunlin University of Science and Technology, Tseng is working as a freelancer, specialising in graphic design, visual identity and branding, publication and book cover, poster, commercial photography, and filmmaking.

PAGE 089

UMA/DESIGN FARM

Founded by art director and designer Yuma Harada in 2007, UMA/design farm works to provide book design, graphic design, exhibition design, space design, and art direction.

PAGE 168-169, 242-243

VACALIEBRES

The visual work of Alberto Vacca Lepri who was born in Genoa, Italy in 1985. Graduated from Fine Arts Academy in Urbino in 2011, vacaliebres has been freelancing with two agencies in Milan and New York.

PAGE 092-095

VIOLAINE & JÉRÉMY

An illustration and graphic design studio based in Paris, Violaine Orsoni and Jérémy Schneider are a team of artistic directors, graphic designers and illustrators. Their projects vary from fabric pattern design to magazine design or brand identity. Their clients include Dior, le Coq Sportif, the National Orchestra of Lorraine, Influencia Magazine, Tiffany and Co. and music labels like Ekler'o'shock.

PAGE 216-217

WANG ZHI-HONG STUDIO

Wang was born in 1975 in Taipei and started his studio in 2000. The six-time winner of Golden Butterfly Awards, Taiwan's highest honour for excellence in book design, has also received international recognitions, including Kaoru Kasai's Choice Award and Excellent Works from Tokyo Type Directors Club Annual Awards.

PAGE 214-215

WING'S ART AND DESIGN STUDIO

Wingsart.net is a collection of ready-made illustrations and design resources by freelance illustrator and graphic designer Christopher Wing King. With nearly two decades of experience, Wing has worked with clients ranging from restaurants, toy companies to blues bands and burlesque troupes.

PAGE 030-031

YONDR STUDIO

The studio of Nathan Yoder. Yoder is an illustrator and designer from Tulsa, Oklahoma. Currently located in Seattle, Washington, he specialises in pen and ink illustration as well as hand lettering and branding.

PAGE 206-207

ZDUNKIEWICZ STUDIO

A small studio based in Warsaw, Poland founded by graphic designer Krzysztof Zdunkiewicz. Focusing on branding and print projects while also working on interactive, app and web projects, Zdunkiewicz is an art director with seven years of experience in advertising and branding. He loves simple and clean ideas, and is obsessed with vintage and black and white projects.

PAGE 058-059

ZEALPLUS

ZEALPLUS is a design studio based in Osaka, Japan. Founded in 2005, the studio specialises in communication design, graphic design and web design.

PAGE 160-161

ACKNOWLEDGEMENTS

WE WOULD LIKE TO THANK ALL THE DESIGNERS AND COMPANIES WHO HAVE INVOLVED IN THE PRODUCTION OF THIS BOOK. THIS PROJECT WOULD NOT HAVE BEEN ACCOMPLISHED WITHOUT THEIR SIGNIFICANT CONTRIBUTION TO THE COMPILATION OF THIS BOOK. WE WOULD ALSO LIKE TO EXPRESS OUR GRATITUDE TO ALL THE PRODUCERS FOR THEIR INVALUABLE OPINIONS AND ASSISTANCE THROUGHOUT THIS ENTIRE PROJECT. THE SUCCESSFUL COMPLETION ALSO OWES A GREAT DEAL TO MANY PROFESSIONALS IN THE CREATIVE INDUSTRY WHO HAVE GIVEN US PRECIOUS INSIGHTS AND COMMENTS. AND TO THE MANY OTHERS WHOSE NAMES ARE NOT CREDITED BUT HAVE MADE SPECIFIC INPUT IN THIS BOOK, WE THANK YOU FOR YOUR CONTINUOUS SUPPORT THE WHOLE TIME.

FUTURE EDITIONS

IF YOU WISH TO PARTICIPATE IN VICTION:ARY'S FUTURE PROJECTS AND PUBLICATIONS, PLEASE SEND YOUR WEBSITE OR PORTFOLIO TO
SUBMIT@VICTIONARY.COM